Seems like a Good Idea

How do you know if it is inspired by the Holy Spirit or your own?

Published by Terry J. Boyle
Copyright © Terry John Boyle 2025.

Unless otherwise noted, all scripture quotations are taken from the Holy Bible, New King James Version Copyright © 1979, 1980, 1982 by Thomas Nelson, Inc.

All rights reserved. No part of this book may be reproduced in any form, stored in a retrieval system, or transmitted in any form by any means—electronic, mechanical, photocopy, recording or otherwise—without the prior written permission of the publisher, except as provided by Australian copyright law.

Words in capitals, or in bold or italics are the emphases of the author Terry Boyle – terryjohnboyle@bigpond.com

Cover & typeset by Carl Butel at Deep Image – carl@deepimage.net.au

Cataloguing-in-Publication data is available from the National Library of Australia.

ISBN 978-0-646-70843-0
eBook ISBN 978-0-646-70876-8

Acknowledgments

I thank my wife, Caroline, for her love, support, and encouragement. I also thank our children Amanda, Felicity, Andrew, Sharon, and their spouses and children for their support.

Our daughter Amanda, for her input, suggestions and encouragement and especially her husband Carl Butel, for the brilliant cover design and internal layout in preparation for printing.

I thank my son Andrew, a Baptist minister, for his encouragement, valuable ideas, wisdom, and doctrinal insight.

I thank the leaders of many denominations for their fellowship and input into my life, especially those associated with A2A over many years.

To all those at Life Ministry Church in Melbourne, where I began ministry, and to all those in Papua New Guinea, where we ministered as Missionaries for many years. Also, those at Centre Church in Lismore, NSW, where we ministered for twenty-one years before semi-retiring to the Gold Coast, Queensland, Australia, where we enjoy fellowship with several churches.

CONTENTS

Introduction

Quotable Quotes on Ideas

1. Inspired or just a good idea
2. It seemed good to the Holy Spirit
3. Does the Holy Spirit convince us?
4. Administering grace for good ideas
5. Can you trust your gut instinct?
6. If it seems good, is it always good?
7. Why do we make mistakes?
8. Believe in the goodness of God
9. Walking the road less travelled
10. Spiritual and natural discernment
11. Is God approachable and flexible?
12. The ripple effect of a good idea
13. Do you desire more of God?
14. Moving forward with confidence
15. A good idea needs the right timing
16. Was Jesus born to be a carpenter?
17. Step out in faith and "Have a go"

Introduction

This is my sixth book. Someone recently asked me, "Where do you get your inspiration?" The short answer is when the Holy Spirit illuminates something from the word of God.

David prayed, *"Open my eyes that I might see wonderous things from your law (word)."* Psalm 119:18. When God opens my eyes to something extraordinary and wonderful in His word, I get excited, and I am like a dog with a bone; I keep gnawing away at it, and sometimes it starts to look like another book.

Why, then, did I write this book?

I was challenged by a daily reading in the "Word for Today" devotional, which referred to Acts 15:28. *"It seemed good to the Holy Spirit and to us."*

The word **"seemed"** troubled me. It caught my attention. I tried to shake it off, but it kept bothering me, so I decided to look into it. It appeared to be far too vague and open-ended to use in conjunction with the Holy Spirit.

Why would something **seem** good to the Holy Spirit? If the Holy Spirit were involved, you would think the phrase would be more definite, like, "The Holy Spirit led us to make

Introduction

this decision."

The Council in Jerusalem (Acts 15) wrote this phrase in a letter to address the issue of Jewish Christians demanding that Gentiles coming to faith in Christ be circumcised and adhere to Jewish customs. It also gave the Gentiles some guidelines.

It only **"seemed"** good. Really! You would think they could do better than that.

My wife and I often say, "That seems like a good idea." Those ideas relate to the everyday decisions we need to make. They come naturally, and we do not consciously consult God about them.

From a Christian perspective, there are times when we have to make monumental decisions, and our good ideas need to be inspired by the Holy Spirit.

However, it raises another question that needs to be answered. As Christians and Church leaders, how do we understand what seemed to be a good idea inspired by the Holy Spirit at the time, only to end up with "egg on our faces" when it did not work out? Was God in it, or was it just a good idea?

Does the word **"seemed"** let us off the hook? If we need the assurance of the Holy Spirit when it comes to significant decisions, how do we go about getting it and then putting it into practice?

Seems Like a Good Idea

Quotable Quotes on Good Ideas

"An idea that is not dangerous is unworthy of being called an idea at all" – Oscar Wilde

"The best way to have a good idea is to have a lot of ideas" – Linus Pauling

"Ideas are easy; it's the execution of ideas that separates the sheep from the goats" – Sue Grafton

"No matter what people tell you, words and ideas can change the world" – Robin Williams

"For good ideas and true innovation, you need human interaction, conflict, argument, debate" – Margaret Hefferman

Seems Like a Good Idea

Chapter 1

Inspired or just a good idea

The first time I preached after joining the ministry team of a large, charismatic church in Melbourne, the associate pastor congratulated me on my sermon and said, "Terry, that was like a breath of fresh air." I cannot remember what I preached but never forgot that compliment.

Mark Twain said, "I can live for two months on a good compliment." However, that compliment I was given will stay with me for the rest of my life.

Good ideas are like a breath of fresh air. We were all created in God's image to have good ideas, and we all have, to some extent, a creative thought process that illuminates our imagination and inspires us to be innovative, just like God.

Our good ideas are the creative juices that inspire us to be inventive and do adventurous things.

They have the breath of life about them

As Christians, the Holy Spirit inspires our good ideas. How can we tell when that happens? They have the breath of life about them. When the Holy Spirit breathes life into those good ideas, they excite and inspire us.

"And the Lord God formed man of the dust of the ground, and breathed into his nostrils the **breath of life***, and man became a living being."* Genesis 2:7.

The breath of life made all the difference, turning physical matter into a living soul. It speaks to us of new life and new beginnings bestowed on us by the Spirit of God.

After His resurrection, Jesus appeared to His disciples and *"He breathed on them and said to them, Receive the Holy Spirit."* John 20:22.

This symbolises a new creation reminiscent of new beginnings (as in Genesis 2:7). Perhaps it was also symbolic of the new covenant of the Spirit now superseding the old Mosaic law.

When the Holy Spirit inspires our ideas. They come alive and impart life and enthusiasm; we want to try them out.

At first, it may be just a puff of life. But no matter how

small that breath of life may seem, we are told not to despise small beginnings. Most of our good ideas start in a small way and build momentum as they develop.

"For who has despised the day of small things?" Zechariah 4:10.

When this was written, the foundation for the temple had been laid (a small beginning), but with the assurance that God would finish it. Most good ideas start in a small way before they develop into something worthwhile.

Like the boy with five loaves and two fish, Jesus took what little he had, blessed it, and distributed it to feed five thousand men besides women and children.

"So, they all ate and were filled, and they took up twelve baskets full of fragments that remained." Matthew 14:20.

No matter how small and insignificant something may seem, God can turn it into a miracle.

Wisdom to implement good ideas

If we are unsure what to do with our good ideas, we should ask God for wisdom and clarity in pursuing them and putting them into practice.

"If any of you lack wisdom, let him ask of God, who gives to all liberally and without reproach, and it will be given him." James 1:5.

We need to know if an idea is worth pursuing or if it is just a fleeting thought with little potential.

Seems Like a Good Idea

Church leaders are pressured to generate innovative ideas to help their churches grow spiritually and numerically. This can lead to mixed results.

An idea is a thought, concept, or hypothesis that will benefit us and others. But we need to discern if it is inspired by God or just an idea.

I like to paint seascapes and landscapes on canvas. When I stand there looking at a blank canvas, I have something in mind and am full of creative thoughts and ideas. But I need to choose and pursue the right one before I paint. Then, as I start painting, I am guided by more ideas until I am satisfied that it is the painting I want to finish. Are they my ideas or inspired by the Holy Spirit? They are probably a combination of both.

Where would we be without good ideas?

Imagine living today without electricity, computers, mobile phones, cars, aeroplanes, the robotic industry, and space exploration, to mention a few. What will be the next exciting new idea resulting in a quantum leap in science and technology? Humans are unique; they are the only species with the ability to have creative new ideas.

I recently listened to Professor Brian Cox explain the vastness of the universe on TV, and I found it fascinating. He asked a philosophical question, "For us as human beings, what does living a finite, fragile life in an infinite, eternal universe mean?" He answered, "Although we are physically insignificant, made up of atoms and molecules, we are the only known beings in the universe to have creative ideas." Like God, we can have creative ideas shaping the present and future.

In his book *Imagine If*, Sir Ken Robinson says, "Creativity – is the ability to generate new ideas and apply them in practice. As young people's challenges proliferate, it is essential to help them develop their unique creative capacities. Like imagination, creativity is not a single power located in one part of the brain but arises from the complex functions of our minds."

The benefit of a collision of ideas

Ideas start within our thinking process. They may come to us as we pray and seek guidance from God.

Sometimes, great ideas are formed by a "collision of ideas." This happens when people from different fields, backgrounds, and cultures come together to discuss their ideas and make decisions based on the best ideas.

Wisdom is gleaned from group discussions, such as in Acts 15, when the leaders met to decide what to do with the Gentiles turning to Christ. They were able to come up with a satisfactory solution.

"Without counsel, plans go awry, but in the multitude of counsellors, they are established." Proverbs 15:22.

This is why God planned for churches to be led by men filled with the Spirit and faith who could work with their elders and other leaders. They combine to create good ideas and make wise decisions. This becomes a safety net that helps us to avoid dictatorial leadership ruling over the flock.

Good ideas may evolve to fulfil a need

Sometimes, good ideas are created to fulfil a need. The classic example is Nehemiah, a cupbearer to the Persian king, who was permitted to visit Jerusalem. However, he told no one what God had put on his heart to do there. While in Jerusalem, he went out by night and viewed all the broken-down walls of the city and its burned gates.

He eventually gathered the Jews, the priests, the nobles and officials and told them what he had been doing and said to them.

> *"You see the distress that we are in, how Jerusalem lies waste, and its gates are burned with fire." "Come let us build the wall of Jerusalem, that we may no longer be a reproach."* Nehemiah 2:13-17.

The walls were in ruins, and he inspired them to start the restoration because of the desperate need to rebuild them and restore the gates. So, they began building and repairing the walls. Despite much opposition, they completed the work in fifty-two days.

The difference between good and bad ideas

Sometimes, when we put into practice what seemed to be a good idea, it is not as good as we thought. It can become an idea we wish we'd never had. Like the person in a hurry who thought it was a good idea to cross over double lines to pass a truck going uphill only to be hit by an oncoming car. As a result of the accident, they ended up as a person with paraplegia. Breaking the road rules was an idea they wished they never had.

Johnny Farnham, an Australian singer, sings the song "It seemed like a good idea" (At the Time). Some lyrics indicate that what seemed like a good idea at the time did not work out because he broke the rules and crossed the line.

> *Did things my way*
> *I've had my say*
> *Sometimes, I crossed that line*
> *But it seemed like a good idea*
> *Seemed like a good idea*
> *At the time.*

A bad idea is to be distinct from a bad day. A bad day is when everything does not go according to plan. That does not mean your idea has failed; it just means you have had a bad day.

Bad ideas usually have poor outcomes. They are often based on flawed assumptions and misguided information. They create more problems than solutions and could be more profitable and beneficial. They may even be dishonest, deceitful, and irresponsible.

However, good ideas have positive outcomes that are usually easy to implement and administer. They are realistic and achievable. They will attract resources to back them up. They will overcome obstacles and be able to solve problems along the way. From a Christian perspective, they should be morally acceptable, ethical, and productive.

Overcome the fear of failure

If you fear failure, you will stop having good ideas.

In an interview, I heard actor George Clooney say, "You learn nothing from success; never, there is nothing you learn from success," "You learn everything from failing." "A fear of failure is what keeps people from doing anything." "When you are older, you may have regrets thinking I could have done that, but I didn't try; if only I had tried."

So, the last thing I want to do is stop anyone from being creative and coming up with good ideas because you fear failure. If something you have implemented as a good idea needs to be fixed, make some adjustments or changes to address the issue. If it is still not working, leave it, move on and start on another good idea.

In the context of a fear of failure, a well-known Bible College lecturer we had as students would continually say, "A car is a lot easier to steer if it is moving." I have never forgotten that and have tried to live by that premise. If something is not working, try to steer it in another direction and make some changes, but never give up. If it is still not working, learn from the failure. Start again with a better idea. You are never defeated until you say you are!

Try, try again

We have all heard the well-known expression, "If at first you don't succeed, try, try again."

It simply means to keep trying, and you will succeed. Many say the first written record of this saying is attributed to Thomas H. Palmer's "Teachers Manual" (1840).

> 'Tis a lesson you should heed,
> Try, try again,
> If, at first, you don't succeed,
> Try, try again.

Some say the expression's essence dates back to Robert the Bruce, a 14th-century leader of Scotland hiding in a cave after being defeated in battle by the English.

While there, he watched a spider trying to spin a web. Each time the spider failed, it would simply try again. The spider so inspired him that he returned to the battlefield and led his troops in a series of victories over the English.

Some of the greatest inventions started with an idea that failed repeatedly. According to his records, Thomas Edison failed 2774 times to design an electric light bulb until he eventually had one work well - what incredible patience and perseverance.

So, I encourage you to keep on having good ideas. Hopefully, they will be like a breath of fresh air, inspired by the Holy Spirit.

Seems Like a Good Idea

Chapter 2

It seemed good to the Holy Spirit

As I quoted in my introduction, *"It seemed good to the Holy Spirit and to us."* Acts 15:28. The word "seemed" troubled me. It is somewhat vague and subject to perception. How do we explain the word seemed in this context?

It only "seemed" good to the Holy Spirit. Really! Is that the best the council at Jerusalem could come up with? You would think they could do better than "seemed" perhaps something more definite like, "The Holy Spirit led us to make this decision."

In this case, the early church had to make an executive decision. They needed to decide how God wanted them to sort out this issue and how they would accept and include the Gentiles.

When it comes to salvation through faith in Christ, the

future of Christianity, the Church, and the entire human race depended upon the outcome of this decision, and all the Council of Jerusalem can say is, "It seemed good to the Holy Spirit and to us."

Is the word "seemed" appropriate?

We know the Holy Spirit does not make mistakes. Were they convinced that the Holy Spirit guided them as they made this decision?

Considering this from a positive point of view, the word "seemed" could allow for human vulnerability and enable them to overcome their embarrassment if things do not work out. It would be appropriate if the direction they gave failed. They could say, "Well, it seemed like a good idea at the time."

The Greek word for "seemed" basically means a subjective opinion. If we were to use "seemed" in a sentence, we would say, "Her eyes seemed to be blue," "He seemed to be ill," or "They seemed to be safe." We think this is true, but it is only what we perceive. We cannot be sure.

Yet, the church leaders did not hesitate to draft this letter in Acts 15 outlining their decision and sending it to the churches.

This is a significant moment in church history. Many early Christians were Jewish and wanted the Gentiles who were non-Jewish to adhere to parts of the Mosaic Law and Jewish customs, especially that of circumcision.

The Gentiles represent all the peoples of the world who were not Jewish. Jesus had already made it clear that the gospel of salvation was to be proclaimed to the whole world.

In the context of Acts 15, Peter declared that to God, there was no difference between Gentiles and Jews. Paul and Barnabas did miracles among the Gentiles because of their faith in Christ. It was also faith alone in Jesus Christ that was sufficient for salvation. Therefore, the Gentile converts were not required to follow aspects of the Law.

After much discussion among these leaders, together with James, it was decided that Gentile believers did not need to adhere to circumcision or other Jewish customs.

However, they were encouraged to abstain from certain practices, such as food sacrificed to idols, eating or drinking blood, strangling animals, and sexual immorality.

Although the word "seemed" used in Acts 15:28 is perceptive to us, it still highlights that this human deliberation was guided by the Holy Spirit and had God's stamp on it.

The leaders believed that the Holy Spirit enabled them to agree to make this decision. But they still had to follow through and implement it.

Maybe it is a good idea to use the word "seemed" more often to allow for our vulnerability in certain decisions that may affect many people's lives instead of the alternative of being emphatic and dogmatic and saying, "God told me."

Using the word "seemed" may be more appropriate, so we take the blame rather than God if things do not work out.

The word "seemed" in the Bible

Let us consider the context of some other references to using the word "seemed" to appreciate an understanding of how it can be interpreted.

Luke addresses his gospel to Theophilus using the same Greek word, saying, *"It seemed good to me also, having had a perfect understanding of all things from the very first, to write to you an orderly account, most excellent Theophilus."* Luke 1:3.

Yes, it seemed reasonable to Luke. He may have started with a good idea that he felt was inspired by the Holy Spirit. Thank God it seemed sensible to Luke to write the inspiring gospel we enjoy today.

The first mention of the word "seemed"

If we consider methods of interpreting the meaning of scripture with the "first-mention principle" of a word or phrase, we need to consider Genesis 19:14.

> *"So, Lot went out and spoke to his sons-in-law, who had married his daughters, and said, "Get up, get out of this place, for the Lord will destroy this city!" But to his sons-in-law, he seemed to be joking."*

To them, he seemed to be joking.

That is one disadvantage of the word "seemed." It cannot be taken as wholly authentic, leaving it up to one's perception.

We see this several times in scripture.

The reaction to Jesus' resurrection

We have a similar situation when some women who had seen the risen Lord went and told the apostles in Luke 24:10-12.

"And their words seemed to them like idle tales, and they did not believe them." But Peter rose and ran to the tomb, and stooping down, he saw the linen clothes lying by themselves; and he departed, marvelling to himself what had happened."

Initially, they had trouble believing them as it seemed they were lying or making it up. But Peter thought, "Well, what if this is true'" and ran to the tomb to find out.

How was Paul perceived in Athens?

The Bible records many adverse reactions to the preaching of the gospel. One such reaction was to Paul, who was provoked in his spirit in Athens and saw how the city was given over to worshipping idols.

"And some said, "What does this babbler want to say?" Others said, "He seems to be a proclaimer of foreign gods because he preached to them Jesus and the resurrection." Acts 17:16-19.

This is what Paul seemed to be doing. Their perception was based on their culture and lack of understanding of the gospel. When we find something hard to understand, we try to work it out according to our perception.

The Theological Implication

Although the word "seemed" in Acts 15:28 may leave the scripture somewhat open to interpretation and our perception, it still affirms that the Holy Spirit played a vital role in leading and guiding the early church.

This was especially evident in critical decisions of doctrine and practice. The Bible, as we know it, is inspired by God.

"All scripture is given by inspiration of God, and is profitable for doctrine, for reproof, for correction, for instruction in righteousness, that the man of God may be complete, thoroughly equipped for every good work." 2 Timothy 3:16-17.

Chapter 3

Does the Holy Spirit convince us?

"It seemed good to the Holy Spirit and to us" (Acts 15:28). This was written by leaders who were led and filled with the Holy Spirit.

The phrase "and to us" indicates that all the apostles, church leaders and elders who gathered in Jerusalem (Acts 15) to discuss this matter were in complete unity and agreement. They seemed convinced that the Holy Spirit led them to make this decision.

This is not just a moment in time; it is not a coincidence or a haphazard decision. It was born out of a new lifestyle as a Christian Community that was developing under the direction of the Holy Spirit according to the New Covenant and not the law of Moses. This was the church in action.

In her book *Pursuing God's Will Together,* Ruth Haley Barton says, "We are more likely to discern God's will when we are in community with others who are also seeking to know and follow Him."

When the Jerusalem council met, it demonstrated how the church desired to be guided by the Holy Spirit to bring unity to the church.

A New Lifestyle

Christians were committed to being "endured with power from on high" (Luke 24:49), which happened initially on the day of Pentecost as those gathered together were filled with the Holy Spirit.

The Bible Project refers to the Book of Acts as the Acts of Jesus and the Holy Spirit. Throughout the Book of Acts, the Apostles and the Holy Spirit work together to affirm the gospel and glorify Christ.

Therefore, the church in Acts 15 had learned a lifestyle that enabled them to come together and make crucial decisions with confirmation from the Holy Spirit as they gathered together through discussion, prayer, fasting and prophecy.

Despite some teething problems, the early Christians had developed a lifestyle through the Spirit that connected them to the risen Lord and the Holy Spirit's moving to bring about signs, wonders, and miracles that glorified Christ.

The early church prioritised the power of the Holy Spirit, working through the apostles, elders, leaders, and believers long before denominational barriers were erected by establishing organisations and institutions like those we have today.

How are we being led today? Does the Holy Spirit have a prominent role in leading us?

Do we need to re-read the Book of Acts to see how vital the Holy Spirit's role was in the church? When we make decisions, can we confidently say, "It seemed good to the Holy Spirit and to us?"

Jesus promised to send the Holy Spirit

Jesus promised to send the Holy Spirit to the disciples as a Helper (not a servant) before He departed.

"I will pray the Father, and He will give you another Helper, that He may abide with you forever – the Spirit of truth, whom the world cannot receive; because it neither sees Him nor knows Him; but you shall know Him, for He dwells with you and shall be in you." John 14:16-17.

The Holy Spirit is called the Spirit of Truth, and He will guide believers into all truth. So, we must accept that the Council in Jerusalem had the Holy Spirit's help to arrive at its decision. The Spirit was leading them. Our problem today is that some church organisations seem to ignore the Helper.

It is to your advantage that I go away

How incredible to think that it would be to our advantage for Jesus to go away.

"It is to your advantage that I go away; for if I do not go away, the

Helper will not come to you; but if I depart, I will send Him to you." John 16:7.

How is this possible? Indeed, nothing could be better than being with Jesus. The disciples have been with him for the last three years. Now, in essence, he is saying, "It is more profitable for you if I go away and send the Holy Spirit to help you."

Jesus, in His physical form, can only be in one place at a time. But the Holy Spirit can help Christians everywhere at any time by anointing their words and convicting people of their need for salvation.

"And when He has come (the helper), He will convict the world of sin, and of righteousness, and of judgment." John 16:8.

We need help presenting the gospel. It is not just our preaching that makes a difference; the anointing of the Holy Spirit convicts people of their need to turn to Christ.

We must realise that the Holy Spirit is a person and learn to access Him. Even if we have a million dollars in the bank, we will still starve unless we access it.

The early church was born of the Spirit

About one hundred and twenty disciples gathered together, waiting for the promise of the Father. This happened when the Holy Spirit came upon the waiting disciples on the day of Pentecost.

"And they were all filled with the Holy Spirit and began to speak with other tongues as the Spirit gave them utterance." Acts 2:4.

On that same day, Peter's preaching convicted many standing by that they had crucified Christ the Lord, the promised Messiah; many repented and were baptised. As a result, a new community of believers was formed.

"Then those who gladly received his word were baptised; about three thousand souls were added to them, and they continued steadfastly in the apostle's doctrine and fellowship, in the breaking of bread and in prayers. Then fear came upon every soul, and many wonders and signs were done through the apostles. Now all who believed were together and had all things in common." Acts 2:41-44.

"It seemed good to the Holy Spirit and to us" signifies that decisions were made as they gathered together to pray, discuss situations, and await confirmation from the Holy Spirit. It became a new way of life for the believers, often confirmed through prophecy or necessity.

The leading of the Holy Spirit

Christians are meant to be led by the Holy Spirit. If we are to be led by the Holy Spirit, we must follow His leading and not expect Him to follow us.

"For as many as are led by the Spirit of God, these are sons of God." Romans 8:14.

This challenges us as we are inclined to do things our way. We need to learn to be led and guided by the Holy Spirit. That is why Jesus sent Him to be our helper. How does this work? The simple answer is that it develops through our relationship with God.

"For you did not receive the spirit of bondage again to fear, but you received the Spirit of adoption by whom we cry out, "Abba, Father." Romans 8:15.

We do not live in fear of failure but by faith in a loving Father willing to help us by leading and guiding us through life.

Men full of the Spirit appointed to serve

They were exciting days as the church increased.

"Through the hands of the apostles, many signs and wonders were done among the people."... "And believers were increasingly added to the Lord, multitudes of both men and women." Acts 5:12-14.

Because of this rapid growth, some believers felt neglected and complained to the apostles that they had missed the daily distribution. So, the apostles gathered the people together to work out a plan to address the issue.

"The twelve summoned the multitude of disciples and said, "We shouldn't leave the word of God and serve tables." "Therefore, brethren, seek out from among you seven men of good reputation, full of the Holy Spirit and wisdom, whom we may appoint over this business." "But we will give ourselves continually to prayer and to the ministry of the word." And the saying pleased the whole multitude." Acts 6:1-5.

They were happy with this decision, and we can only assume that the Holy Spirit guided them in choosing the right men, who were of a good reputation and full of the Holy Spirit and wisdom, to help with the daily distribution to people in need.

These were good men, and it was not long before some developed into gifted ministries, the most notable being Philip.

The Ministry of Philip

Philip became an evangelist.

He went to the City of Samaria and preached Christ in the city. A revival broke out, and many came to believe in Christ. Others were healed and delivered from demonic oppression (Acts 8:4-8).

After preaching to crowds, Philip left the revival, being directed by an angel to speak to one man, an Ethiopian eunuch who had great authority under Candace, the queen of Ethiopia.

This took place on the road between Jerusalem and Gaza through the desert. The Holy Spirit led him to preach Christ to this man. Then, he led him to faith in Christ and baptised him in water.

Philip is most noted for his supernatural mode of transport via the Spirit: "The Spirit of the Lord caught Philip away." He was found in Azotus (also known as Ashdod), about 50 kilometres away, depending on his location. It would have been an arduous journey on foot that would have taken several hours. Philip was undoubtedly walking and living in the power of the Holy Spirit.

"Now when they came up out of the water, the Spirit of the Lord caught Philip away, so that the eunuch saw him no more, and he went on

his way rejoicing. But Philip was found in Azotus. And passing through he preached in all the cities till he came to Caesarea". Acts 8:39-40.

Interestingly, Philip and others chosen to serve on tables were full of the Holy Spirit, wisdom and faith. So, this new community of Church leaders, ministries, and believers worked together and relied on one another and the Holy Spirit to proclaim the gospel.

The Holy Spirit leads in mysterious ways

I had been on a Ministry trip to PNG, and when I came back to Australia, I was burdened with a vision that seemed to be inspired by the Holy Spirit to establish a Bible College in PNG to train national leaders.

I wrote a plan for the college listing twelve strategic points necessary for such a college.

I reluctantly shared this outline with my wife, Caroline. She was not impressed, as we had just built our first-ever house in Melbourne, Australia. Her first reaction was, "Over my dead body." She finally relented and said, "If God is in it, He can make the next move. So, I agreed, put the draft plan in my office desk drawer and waited.

At the time, I was on the ministry team of this thriving Charismatic Church in Melbourne. These were exciting days as God poured out His Holy Spirit, and we saw people saved, healed, and delivered.

After about nine months, the senior pastor, the late Hal

Oxley, decided to go overseas on a holiday and ministry trip, and I was left in charge of opening his mail.

I opened a letter from the late John Pasterkamp, a church leader and missionary in Port Moresby. He asked Hal if he had a suitable couple to release to come and start a Bible College.

This letter was like a breath of fresh air. He listed ten out of the twelve points I had put in my office desk drawer. I had already met John on my previous trip to PNG, and we were of a kindred spirit. I was excited but had to convince my wife and Hal that this was God.

There was no denying that God had made the next move. They did not take much convincing; it was apparent, and after prayer and prophetic words of confirmation, we were on our way. We initially went for one year but ended up staying for six years.

The rest is history. It was a great success and impacted the nation of PNG as God poured out His Spirit during these years.

However, there were obstacles, and it was not all plain sailing. But at the time, "It seemed good to the Holy Spirit and to us." It had God's stamp on it. As they say, "The proof is in the pudding."

Abiding in Christ to be fruitful

Anything born of the Spirit will bear the fruit of the Spirit, providing that we are walking in step with the Holy Spirit. Without the Spirit, we labour in vain.

"Unless the Lord builds the house, we labour in vain who build it." Psalm 127:1.

Jesus implied that if we want to be successful, we should do nothing of ourselves or without Him by our side. He describes it this way.

"Abide in Me, and I in you. As the branch cannot bear fruit of itself unless it abides in the vine, neither can you unless you abide in Me." "I am the vine, you are the branches, He who abides in Me, and I in him, bears much fruit; for without Me you can do nothing." John 15:4-5.

How do we abide in Christ and He in us? By being led by the Holy Spirit. Therefore, we need to walk in step with the Holy Spirit.

Chapter 4

Administering grace for good ideas

Administering grace is desperately needed if we are to implement good ideas. Grace enables us to step out in faith and experiment without fearing failure.

The administration of grace helped Paul minister to the Gentiles, transitioning them from the demands of the law to embrace the gospel of grace.

In writing to the Ephesians, the apostle Paul says, *"Surely you have heard of the **administration** of God's grace."* Ephesians 3:1 (NIV).

When we hear the word administration, we usually think of managing or overseeing an operation, function, business, institution, or church. However, Paul claims he was called to administer God's grace to the Gentiles.

"For this reason, I, Paul, the prisoner of Christ for the sake of you

Gentiles – For surely you have heard of the **administration** *of God's grace that was given to me for you, that is the mystery made known to me by revelation, as I have already written briefly."* Ephesians 3:1-2 (NIV).

The word **administration** comes from the Greek *oikonomia*, which can also be translated as **stewardship, management, or dispensation**. Different translations of the Bible use all of these words, but in this context, I am highlighting the NIV.

In the above scripture, he is writing to the church at Ephesus, which was mainly composed of Gentile believers. Paul implies he has become a prisoner of Christ to administer God's grace to the Gentiles. He is convinced this is a unique role and responsibility entrusted to him to take the gospel of grace to the Gentiles (non-Jewish peoples). He sees this as a gift, not something he has earned or achieved by his merit.

This was more than just a good idea that Paul thought up to reach the Gentiles for Christ. It was ordained by God and inspired by the Holy Spirit.

We see this unfolding in Acts 15:10-11 which addresses the conflict in which Jewish Christians demanded that the Gentile Christians be circumcised according to Jewish tradition.

This is a classic example of God's grace being applied to this situation to help them reach their decision. God's grace overruled the law and Jewish customs. So, they declared that it seemed good to the Holy Spirit and to us to lay no other burden but these necessary things. It was assuring the believers that the grace of God saved them.

"Now, therefore, why do you test God by putting a yoke on the neck of the disciples, which neither our fathers nor we were able to bear? But we believe that through the grace of our Lord Jesus Christ, we shall be saved in the same manner as they." Acts 15:10-11.

So, the administration of God's grace refers to how grace was administered in the early church to nullify the legalistic application of the Mosaic law and some Jewish customs.

Grace upon grace

"And of His fulness, we have all received, and grace for grace (or grace upon grace). John 1:16.

We are saved by grace and faith in Jesus Christ, but grace is not a one-off experience through salvation. Grace is ongoing, and His grace upon grace enables us to be transformed into the image of Christ.

"For the law was given through Moses, but grace and truth came through Jesus Christ." John 1:17.

Moses gave law upon law, but it changed nothing. No matter how hard we try to keep it,

The law condemned us and showed us our desperate need for a saviour and His grace. Now, through Christ and His grace upon grace, we are being changed into the image of Christ without guilt and condemnation.

In my book *But for the Gace of God Go I*, I devote a chapter to

"Grace in the Book of Acts," expanding this issue and others concerning God's grace. I also include stories of how a fresh understanding of grace changed my life and ministry.

Can grace and effort work together?

Theologically, grace and effort seem to oppose one another or are at opposite ends of the spectrum. To embrace grace is to move away from effort, and to apply effort is to move away from grace.

If we apply effort to good ideas, it is all about getting busy implementing those ideas. If it is about grace, it's about relaxing and not getting into "works of righteousness." Grace can give us the impression that we do not have to do anything.

I like what Dallas Willard says, "Grace is not opposed to effort; it is opposed to earning. Earning is an attitude. Effort is an action."

When initiating good ideas, there is no reason why grace and effort cannot work together to complement one another.

Yes, we are saved by grace; it is the gift of God that is to be received by faith. There is nothing we have to do; it has been done for us through Christ. We have a responsibility to administer this grace. His grace enables us to experiment with good ideas, which often require some effort on our part.

A mystery now revealed in Christ

Paul calls this administration of grace a mystery (once hidden but now revealed). It was a hidden mystery in other ages, but the Holy Spirit has revealed it to him. The message of salvation now comes through grace and faith in Christ. He is responsible for administering this grace and explaining it to the Gentiles.

A mystery is not something that can never be known but is hidden because it is not fully revealed or understood. Under the old covenant, salvation revolved around keeping the law and the sacrifices God required to forgive sins.

This gospel of grace was embraced by the Gentiles and spread rapidly throughout the Roman Empire.

"And without controversy great is the mystery of Godliness: God was manifest in the flesh, justified in the Spirit, seen by angels, preached among the Gentiles, believed on in the world, received up into Glory." 1 Timothy 3:16.

This now means that everyone, Jew, Gentile, and whatever nation one belongs to, has access to God through Christ. It demonstrates God's mercy and grace in redeeming humanity from the effects of sin and death.

In his book *What's So Amazing About Grace*, Phillip Yancey says, "The church is not a museum for saints, but a hospital for sinners." He highlights how grace should be administered to those who are hurting and in need, emphasising the church's role in offering grace, not judgment.

Justified through faith in Christ

One fundamental doctrine we all need to embrace is, "The

just shall live by faith." We do not have to do anything to impress God or others, nor do we have to perform or conform to a set of rules to justify our salvation. Galatians 3: 11 states,

"But that no one is justified by the law in the sight of God is evident, for "the just shall live by Faith."

Most Christians today understand this truth and are free from the Mosaic Law. However, some still make their own rules and practice things that become legalistic. Many Christians think that the harder you try, the more you fast and pray, the more likely you are to hear from God. I have been down this path.

While working on the mission field in Papua New Guinea, I decided to seek God through prayer and fasting. It was not my original intention, but I ended up fasting for forty days with no food but plenty of water, lemonade, fruit juice and coffee. It was a gruelling but rewarding experience. The big lesson I learned was that fasting is a great discipline, but you do not have to fast to hear from God, for He is constantly with us and in us through the power of the Holy Spirit. I elaborate on this in my book Hungry for God.

Pressure to perform

When I began full-time ministry, I was on the team of a large, charismatic church. The senior pastor had been a colonel in the Australian Army and a successful businessman before entering the ministry. I was always under pressure to perform. I kept a scorecard in my mind of successes and failures, with credits and demerits. I was forever in the deficit column and needed help measuring up to the set standards. I felt I always had to try harder.

It is easy to fall into the perfectionist trap. Thomas Curran, an associate professor at the London School of Economics, describes himself as a "recovering perfectionist." In his book *The Perfectionist Trap*, he says, "Much perfectionism comes from worrying about not being "good enough" or that "I don't belong."

We must be careful not to fall into this or any legalistic trap that dampens our faith and enthusiasm for following Christ. It is futile even to try to make ourselves perfect. There is only one perfect person, and that person is God Himself.

We are saved by grace through faith in Christ; it is a gift from God. It is never dependent upon our works lest we boast. (Ephesians 2:8)

What are we administering? Are you and I administering the law, legalism, condemnation, judgment, or the grace of God?

Seems Like a Good Idea

Chapter 5

Can you trust your gut instinct?

"Gut instinct" or intuitive decision-making is the ability to instantly understand something without considering other people's opinions or taking time to think it over; it is your inner feeling about something.

As I said in my introduction, my wife and I often say, "That seems like a good idea." Those ideas relate to everyday decisions we need to make. They come naturally, and we do not consciously consult God about them. It is our "gut instinct" that we rely on to make those decisions.

However, can we trust our gut instinct? It is usually an excellent guide we should value and learn to listen to it, but it is not foolproof. From a Christian perspective, we must sense that the Holy Spirit inspires us. It is also wise to bounce it off others as a safety check.

Gut instinct and hearing His voice

Together with gut instinct, we need to hear the voice of the Holy Spirit Today. First, His voice will always be in harmony with God's word.

Our challenge is to hear the inner witness of his voice in our hearts and minds. The most significant barrier for us not to listen to His voice is for us to harden our hearts by disobeying when we do.

"Today, if you will hear His voice. Do not harden your hearts as in the rebellion." Hebrews 3;15.

So, if we learn anything from history, we go back to the children of Israel in the wilderness, where they hardened their hearts and rebelled against God.

How do we relate to that today? Well, it was written to the early church to warn them not to harden their hearts by ignoring or rebelling against God by refusing to heed His voice. These things are written as warnings and also examples for us today.

The art of discerning His voice?

How do we hear His voice today? The simple answer is through prayer, His word, the gifts of the Holy Spirit, the church, ministries, and other believers.

If He spoke through a megaphone, sounded a siren, added flashing lights and made a loud verbal announcement, we would easily recognise His voice. But as you know, it does not happen that way.

But it may be easier than you think!

In her book *Discerning the Voice of God,* Pricilla Shirer says, "As you seek to hear from God, expect Him to speak. Trust that you can discern His voice. He wants you to know His will even more than you desire."

I remember an American minister who knew the art of discerning the voice of the Holy Spirit. He moved powerfully in a word of knowledge and faith through operating spiritual gifts.

When asked how he could be sure he was hearing the voice of the Holy Spirit, he found it hard to explain. He said, "It is different for everyone, but it was an inner knowing for him." He said, "When you know that you know that you know it is His voice because you know.

The Apostles heard His voice clearly

We see this happening as the Holy Spirit speaks directly to the Apostles on several occasions, guiding and directing them by giving specific instructions.

"Then the Spirit told Philip, "Go near and overtake this chariot." Acts 8:29.

"While Peter thought about the vision, the Spirit said to him, "Behold, three men are seeking you. Arise, therefore, go down and go with them, doubting nothing for I have sent them." Acts 10:19-20.

"As they ministered to the Lord and fasted, the Holy Spirit said, "Now, separate for Me Barnabas and Saul for the work for which I have

called them." Acts 13:2.

"Now, when they had gone through Phrygia and the region of Galatia, they were forbidden by the Holy Spirit to preach the word in Asia." Acts 16:6-7.

Although they heard the voice of the Holy Spirit clearly, we need to know precisely how this was happening. They were able to recognise it.

Do we recognise the Master's voice and listen intently to it? In July 1900, Emile Berliner, the inventor of the Gramophone, obtained North American Rights and registered his company's famous logo. It showed the friendly little dog listening, spellbound, to a gramophone with the slogan "His Master's Voice."

From a personal point of view, we often know within us how the Holy Spirit speaks to us. We may become familiar with that way, which will vary from person to person depending on what we have experienced.

There is an inner witness of the Holy Spirit, which for some may be quiet and gentle; for others, it may be more of a compelling urgency or serene and peaceful. This may also depend upon the circumstances we are encountering at the time.

We must recognise His voice in whatever way He speaks so the Spirit can lead us. If we do not know His voice, how can the Spirit of God lead us and direct us through life?

"For as many as are led by the Spirit of God, these are the sons of God. For you did not receive the spirit of bondage again to fear, but you received the Spirit of adoption by whom we cry out, "Abba, Father." Romans 8:14-16.

As many as are led by the Spirit are God's sons (and daughters). He expects us to be led by His Spirit, which is enhanced by having a personal relationship with Him as our loving Father. We cry out, "Abba Father" (Dear Daddy). He wants to relate to us as a loving father, not an austere judge, but as a father who wants to care for His children.

My experience of hearing a still, small voice

In my book *Hungry for God*, I shared how I drove up into the Hills outside Port Moresby on the last day of a forty-day fast in PNG to see if God would manifest Himself to me somehow.

I walked around the bush, yelling, "Where are you, God? Show yourself to me; strike some trees with lightning, do something, so I know it is you."

Then, I heard a still small voice within me say, "Here I Am," and I knew it was God. God refers to Himself as the "I Am" which speaks of His eternal existence. I thought of how Elijah stood at the cave entrance where he was hiding, and God manifested himself to him.

"And behold the Lord passed by, and a great and strong wind tore into the mountains and broke the rocks in pieces before the Lord, but the Lord was not in the wind; and after the wind an earthquake, but the Lord was

not in the earthquake, and after the earthquake a fire, but the Lord was not in the fire, and after the fire a still small voice."... "What are you doing here, Elijah?" 1 Kings 19:11-12.

God was not in those spectacular manifestations but in a still, small voice. Sometimes, we expect God to speak to us miraculously; of course, He can do that, but my experience has been that it is usually through his still, small voice or the inner witness of the Holy Spirit.

God said to Elijah, "What are you doing here?" This indicates he may not have been in God's will at the time. He had to be redirected by that still small voice, and so do we at times.

I became familiar with that still small voice and made a habit of being sensitive to it. We had been praying for baby Saua in our church in Port Moresby. She had been diagnosed with an inoperable brain tumour. Her head was swollen on one side, and she had been to Australia for treatment, but they could do nothing for her.

One morning in our church service, I heard a small voice within me say, "You need to anoint baby Saua with oil and pray for her to be healed."

I was sitting next to the late John Pasterkamp, who was about to get up to take communion. John told the congregation what I had just shared with him and called the parents forward with baby Saua. You could feel faith rise in the meeting. We prayed and anointed her with oil.

In a matter of weeks, the swelling disappeared, and further

scans showed no sign of the Tumour. It was a miracle. Saua grew up as an average child into adulthood. The last time I heard of Saua, she was about twenty years old and living an ordinary life. Praise God!

Through prayer, fasting, and prophecy

In Acts 15:28, "It seemed good to the Holy Spirit and to us." The decision had come through collective wisdom as the leaders and elders gathered as a council in Jerusalem to discuss the matter.

But it was more than just wisdom from those gathered together. The Spirit confirmed it. How did this happen? We are not told in detail, but if we look at a similar scripture, we gain insight into what may have happened.

At Antioch, certain prophets and teachers had gathered to pray and fast.

"As they ministered to the Lord and fasted, the Holy Spirit said, "Now separate to Me Barnabas and Saul for the work for which I have called them."… "So, being sent out by the Holy Spirit." Acts 13:2-4.

"The Holy Spirit said." How did the Holy Spirit speak? They were hearing the Holy Spirit's voice, but in this case, it is not clear. We can only assume it was through a prophetic word or that one or more of those who gathered spoke these words, as the Holy Spirit does not usually speak and give direction without a mouthpiece.

Some guidelines for hearing His voice –

These points are worth considering when trying to discern the voice of the Holy Spirit.

1. **A still-small voice**
   The inner witness of the Holy Spirit within us.

2. **Collective wisdom**
   As leaders, pastors, and elders gather together to discuss situations.

3. **Prayer, fasting, prophecy and discernment**
   We are seeking God together for wisdom and guidance.

4. **Biblical Foundations**
   We are consulting Scripture to build decisions on a Biblical foundation.

5. **Unity and peace**
   That the decision is made out of unity and that it brings peace and satisfaction.

6. **Open communication**
   That all opinions and ideas are given equal hearing for open discussion.

7. **A step of faith to act upon it**
   Step out in faith and act on the decision by implementing and monitoring it.

Chapter 6

If it seems good, is it always good?

We all have what seems to be good ideas, but are they always good? We usually think so. Otherwise, we would not pursue them and put them into practice.

Do we ever bother to question the source of our good ideas? Who inspired them? Was it just us? Was it God? Was it the devil, surely not, or was it?

Some ideas that seem to be right can even lead to death. *"There is a way that seems right to man. But its end is the way of death."* Proverbs 14:12.

It is a sobering scripture suggesting that something we think is good, reasonable, and right can lead to death. It happened to Adam and Eve in the Garden of Eden. What seemed to be a good idea led to sin and death, which came upon the entire human race. The devil deceived them.

Lies lead to deception

The devil twisted the truth in the Garden of Eden by lying and tempting Eve and Adam to eat fruit from the tree God had told them not to eat from.

The lie was subtle, and it seemed to be feasible. But the devil undermined the word of God by giving Eve the impression that God was reasonable and would look the other way if she did eat from the tree.

"Has God indeed said, "You shall not eat of every tree of the garden…(but if you do) "You shall not surely die." (God loves you too much to let that happen). Genesis 3:1 and 4. The brackets are my inferences.

Jesus describes the devil as the father of lies.

"When the devil speaks, He speaks a lie; he speaks from his own resources, for he is a lie and the father of it." John 8:44.

The devil is a subtle, almost believable liar, and that is why we can be so easily deceived. Surely, Adam and Eve could tell they were being lied to. What were they thinking?

In his book *Blink: The Power of Thinking without Thinking*, Malcolm Gladwell says, "Truly successful decision-making relies on a balance between deliberate and instructive thinking." How intuition should be balanced with deliberate reasoning.

It appeared good to their senses

For Adam and Eve, what the devil said seemed good because it appealed to their senses.

"So, when the woman saw that the tree was good for food, that it was pleasant to the eyes, and a tree desirable to one wise, she took of its fruit and ate. She also gave it to her husband with her, and he ate." Genesis 3:4-6.

We all struggle with this kind of temptation at times: the temptation to gratify the desires of the flesh. John describes it as all that is in the world that does not come from God.

"For all that is in the world – the lust of the flesh, the lust of the eyes, and the pride of life – is not of the Father but is of the world." 1 John 2:16.

James describes fleshly temptations so well. He uses the words "drawn away by our desires and enticed." This is what happened to Adam and Eve.

They were tempted by their desires, enticed, and drawn away from God by believing the lies of the devil, and so can we if we succumb to temptation. The result for humanity was sin and death.

"But each one is tempted when he is drawn away by his desires and enticed. Then when desire has conceived, it gives birth to sin, and sin, when it is fully grown, brings forth death." James 1:14-15.

Resist the temptation

When the devil tempted Jesus, he resisted every temptation by quoting scripture to contradict Satan's lies by saying, *"It is written."* (Matthew 4:1-11).

Most of our temptations are subtle and cause us to disobey God. By resisting, Jesus was able to overcome the temptation. We need to do the same. The Bible tells us that with every temptation, there will also be a way of escape. God promises to help us if we are willing to obey Him.

"No temptation has overtaken you except such as common to man, but God is faithful, who will not allow you to be tempted beyond what you are able, but with the temptation will also make the way of escape, that you may be able to bear it." 1 Corinthians 10:13.

The devil is not likely to go away if we plead with him. We must put our foot down and resist him by standing on the word.

James 4:7 says, *"Resist the devil, and he will flee from you."* This is what Jesus did, and we need to practice it.

Our hearts can deceive us

Do we know our hearts? *"The heart is deceitful above all things and desperately wicked." Who can know it?"* Jeremiah 17:9.

Can we deceive ourselves? Is this possible for a Christian? A few other scriptures may convince you.

"If we claim to be without sin, we deceive ourselves" (1 John 1:8), *"If we hear the word and do not do it, we deceive ourselves"* (James 1:22), *"We deceive ourselves If we think we are wise according to this age"* (1 Corinthians 3:18).

We need to have an overall knowledge of the word of God as to what is likely to entice and deceive us.

When it comes to deception, we also battle against *"Lying spirits"* (1 Tim 4:1) and *"Evil doers and imposters"* (2 Timothy 3:13).

In his book, *The Abolition of Man*, C. S. Lewis says, "Aristotle says that education aims to make the pupil like and dislike what he ought." Are we educated enough to know the difference?

Deception can infiltrate the church

Deception infiltrated the early church, leading to the apostle Paul's dissatisfaction with the Galatians. He is not impressed and challenges them by rebuking them for being deceived doctrinally.

"O foolish Galatians! Who has bewitched you that you should not obey the truth?" Galatians 3:1.

Bewitched is a strong word; it means you have been hoodwinked and deceived by someone who has twisted the truth, and you have been foolish enough to believe it.

This is over the same issue as in Acts 15, where many of the Jewish Christians were demanding that the Gentiles be circumcised according to the law and their traditions. Paul even confronts Peter, who is sympathetic to the Galatians at the time.

Paul encourages them to realise they are justified by faith

in Christ, not the law; it is by grace that they are saved. Now, he tells them to walk in the Spirit and not the lusts of the flesh (Galatians 5).

He reminds them they are under a new Covenant (or way of life). Some Christians get side-tracked by what they think is right and will argue and become dogmatic in defence of what seems right.

Deception in the last days

Deception will be rampant in the last days before Christ's return. Hardly a day goes by without us receiving a phone call or something via the internet that is a scam.

> *"So, the great dragon was cast out, that serpent of old called the Devil and Satan, who deceives the whole world; he was cast to the earth, and his angels were cast out with him."* Revelation 12:9.

The devil has not changed his tactics; he is out to deceive the whole world. As you read this, millions of people are being ripped off by deceptive scams that sound so good.

Christians can be deceived

Some years ago, we got caught up in a scam led by a man posing as a Christian. This man and his get-rich-quick scheme deceived thousands of leaders, churches, and Christians.

His name was Noah Musingku, and he was from Bougainville, PNG. It was a deceptive investment scheme that started before the year 2000 and may continue in some areas today.

Like most of these schemes, those involved in the early days did very well and were returned enormous profits from their investments. But that was the lure to get the multitudes on the bandwagon, and it worked. But after a while, they did not receive their promised return. As they say, "If it seems too good to be true, then it probably is."

Sadly, this scheme deceived mainly Christians to the extent that some church leaders even promoted it. I met Noah briefly at a church where he was able to encourage his scheme. I tried to talk to him, but he was elusive, had no eye contact, and kept walking away.

His last recorded interview was in 2020. He had evaded arrest and was hiding in his remote home area of Tonu in Bougainville. Some photos were published of him surrounded by several armed bodyguards. One of the photos showed him wearing a brass crown. He had re-christened himself as King David of the Kingdom of Papaala. (thought to be a traditional name for Bougainville).

Many years ago, I was on a return visit to PNG with Barry Winton to minister in Bougainville where Barry had been a missionary for many years. We wanted to travel down to Tonu and had to obtain passes to do so while ministering in Buka. These passes were needed to supposedly get us through the Bougainville Revolutionary Army (BRA) roadblocks at the Bougainville Copper Mine which was a stronghold for the (BRA). They had been at war with PNG trying to gain independence for Bougainville. However, we could not find anyone willing to drive us down through the jungle and the roadblocks to get there. No one volunteered. We later found out what we had suspected, that Noah had close links to the BRA, and much of the money from the scheme supported that cause.

As the scripture says, *"Even the very elect of God can be deceived."* (Matthew 24:24).

I was recently deceived by scammers

I recently had a call from someone who claimed to be a detective working for the Fraud Squad to say that money had been scammed from our bank account. He gave me his name and ID number and told me to ring 000 to confirm this was authentic. So, I did, and 000 confirmed his identity. He then asked me to ring the bank number on my credit card so the bank could confirm the missing amount. So, I did, and they confirmed what he had told me. He suspected that it was an inside job in the bank, and they wanted to use me to trace where it was coming from. We had been to a branch the day before, and they had checked something on our credit card, so we were suspicious. He said that to find out who was behind it, you need to transfer money from your account to an account the scammers had been using. He guaranteed that the fraud squad would cover any loss of money. He gave me a code word and said I would be working undercover for the fraud squad. So, I did make the transfer.

About 10 minutes later, I had a call from the bank fraud division headquarters in Sydney. They had blocked this transfer and asked me about it because they felt it was suspicious.

If it seems good, is it always good?

When I told them the whole story, they assured me this was the work of scammers. I was so angry with myself for falling for this scam but so thankful for the Lord's intervention through the bank. How they used 000 and the bank number is being investigated.

So, what seems good is only sometimes good. Jesus warned us that deception would be prevalent in the last days.

Seems Like a Good Idea

Chapter 7

Why do we make mistakes?

Why do we make mistakes? There are many reasons why. We are not invincible; we are only human and battle with worldly desires, selfish ambitions, pride, and fleshly gratifications, to mention a few.

We are in a battle between the flesh and the Spirit. Sometimes, we get confused about what is just a fleshly good idea and what is of the Spirit.

The phrase *"It seemed good to the Holy Spirit and to us."* (Acts 15:28) can have a positive side to it. It may let us off the hook when we are uncertain about our course of action.

As I said, "seemed" allows us to speculate or perceive that the decision is correct but does not hold us accountable if it does not work out.

Not that the Holy Spirit ever makes a mistake.

But what about us? If it initially seemed okay but did not work out, we can admit that it only "seemed" good at the time. This allows for failure and helps us recover from our mistakes. God is gracious and enables us to heal, overcome our disappointment and embarrassment and move on.

God will never define us by our mistakes. Like the story of the "Prodigal Son" who made terrible mistakes. When he returned home, his father was waiting, ready to forgive, restore and celebrate his return. Not like his elder brother, who was prepared to condemn him and remind everyone of his mistakes. (Luke 15:11-21).

I suspect there may be a few elder brothers in the church today who define us by our mistakes and are ready to point them out to us and others.

What was Peter thinking?

Peter thought it was a good idea at the time when they came to arrest Jesus to take out his sword and cut off the servant of the High Preist's ear. But Jesus rebuked him and told him to put away his sword.

It was a big mistake for Peter, and he could have been arrested and convicted of attempted murder. Was Peter aiming at his head or his ear? Whatever the case, maybe Jesus took away any evidence that could have convicted him by healing the servant's ear. (Luke 22:49-51).

We can see a similarity here: when Jesus died on the cross, His shed blood took away any evidence of our sins. No one, including the devil, can convict or condemn us. There is no more evidence against us. This is why we have scriptures like – *"There is therefore no condemnation to those who are in Christ Jesus, who do not walk according to the flesh, but according to the Spirit."* Romans 8:1.

I thought it was a good idea at the time

After graduating from Bible College in Adelaide, we moved to Melbourne to allow my wife Caroline to finish her degree in Agricultural Science, which she had almost finished at Melbourne University before meeting me.

While in Melbourne, I was looking for ministry and was convinced that the Holy Spirit was leading me to Launceston, Tasmania, where we knew a pastor was looking for a replacement. So, one long weekend, I thought flying down to meet this pastor and investigate the possibilities was a good idea at the time.

I had a strange experience as the plane touched down in Launceston and was still on the runway; I knew in my spirit that this was not right. But how could I get it so wrong when it seemed so right? My desperate desire to enter ministry overshadowed what God wanted me to do.

I graciously spent a lovely weekend in Tasmania, but again, something strange happened. When I flew back and the plane circled over Melbourne, I knew it was the place God wanted me to be. It was a work of grace because I did not like Melbourne and was looking for a way out.

A few weeks later, I received a phone call that changed my life and shaped my ministry. The senior pastor of a thriving charismatic church in Melbourne rang and invited me to join the full-time ministry team. God was gracious and redirected me.

What are our motives?

We must have the right motives if we are to avoid making mistakes. Sometimes, our pride and selfish ambitions lead us astray. Are we here to serve or be served?

In their book, *The Boy Crisis*, Warren Farell and John Gray write about the challenges young men face in modern Western culture. They say, "The fathers of the past generation had an attitude of "I exist; therefore, I serve." They believe today's generation seems to carry the attitude of "I exist; therefore, I deserve." However, going through life feeling like you always deserve a good outcome may be filled with frustration and disappointment.

James 4:1-6 indicates that we can have the wrong motives when we pray. It implies we do not get answers to prayer, firstly because we do not bother to pray, secondly because we have selfish motives, and thirdly because of our pride.

Maybe we feel God owes us a favour because we deserve it. If we have the wrong motive, that can be a recipe for making mistakes. Remember, Jesus said He came to serve.

Sometimes, we are not on the same page

"For My thoughts are not your thoughts, Nor, are your ways My ways, says the Lord." Isaiah 55:8.

We are often on a different page to God. This usually happens when we make our interests and desires our priority in life. But God knows what we need to pursue, which sometimes differs from what we imagine.

"For I know the thoughts I think towards you, says the Lord, thoughts of peace and not of evil, to give you a future and a hope." Jeremiah 29:11.

God has our best interest at heart; even when we think we have it right, he knows what is best for our future.

Some years ago, when we were pastoring in Lismore, NSW, my wife and I had the opportunity to attend a conference with a group of Australian pastors at "Willow Creek Community Church" in Chicago, USA.

It was a megachurch that was reaching thousands for Christ. Its "Seeker-sensitive model" church style effectively worked brilliantly for them.

We came back to Australia with plenty of enthusiasm. It seemed like a good idea for our church, and thinking the Holy Spirit inspired it, we decided to implement it.

We were able to unearth some hidden talent in our church for notable productions that fit this "seeker-sensitive model" designed to appeal to the unsaved. However, although we had a measure of success, it was not as fruitful as we thought.

It was hard work, and only a short time before everyone involved started to wear out. So, we decided it was not a good fit for our church and canned the programme.

But it seemed right at the time. How did we get it wrong? Maybe we failed to administer it correctly.

However, we did not dwell on it or let it get the better of us. By His grace, God enabled us to recover, shake off the dust of disappointment and failure, and move on.

We learnt from this experience and tried to develop a habit as leaders and elders of having a retreat at the end of the year to pray and plan for the following year.

"Trust in the Lord with all your heart and lean not on your own understanding; in all your ways acknowledge Him, and He shall direct your paths." Proverbs 3:5-6.

Sometimes, the disciples got it wrong

Not that I mean to pick on him, but bold, impetuous Peter, the only other man apart from Jesus to walk on water, got it right and wrong on several occasions.

Peter was the first to have a revelation that Jesus was the Christ (Messiah), the son of the living God. Jesus complimented him for getting it right.

"He said to them, "But who do you say that I am?" Simon Peter answered and said, *"You are the Christ, the Son of the living God." Jesus answered and said to him, "Blessed are you, Simon Bar-Jonah, for flesh and blood has not revealed this to you, but My Father who is in*

Why do we make mistakes?

heaven." Matthew 16:17-18.

So, Peter was spot on; he got that right, and the Spirit revealed it to him, but a few verses later, we read that he got it all wrong.

"From that time, Jesus began to show to His disciples that He must go to Jerusalem, and suffer many things from the elders and chief priests and scribes, and be killed and raised the third day. Then Peter took Him aside and began to rebuke Him, saying, "Far be it from You, Lord; this shall not happen to you." But He turned and said to Peter, "Get behind Me, Satan!" Matthew 16:21-23.

Peter sure got it wrong when Jesus said to him, "Get behind Me, Satan." Peter was influenced by his own emotions and acted impulsively because he did not like the thought of Jesus being killed. He did not want to lose Jesus.

When I first got saved, the pastor (Tony Smits) who led me to the Lord was a great Bible teacher, and I learned so much under his ministry. One day, he said, "Terry, I think God is calling me to Papua New Guinea." I freaked out at the thought of losing him and said, "I think your ministry is needed here in Australia." I was only thinking of myself. He never went to PNG. But guess who God called to go to PNG some years later? Yes, that was me.

Peter continued to fluctuate between getting it right and wrong. When someone pointed him out as one of the disciples when Jesus was arrested to stand trial, Peter denied knowing Him.

However, when the Holy Spirit was poured out on the day of Pentecost, the believers appeared to be drunk with wine. Peter boldly and courageously stood up and preached about Christ, explaining that they were not drunk but filled with the Holy Spirit that was poured out just as the prophet Joel had said it would be in the last days. As a result, about three thousand souls came to faith in Christ. Peter sure got it right that time.

But it wasn't just Peter who had trouble getting it right. There was another occasion where James and John got it wrong. They had sent messengers to a Samaritan village to get them to prepare for Jesus, but they would not receive Him.

"When His disciples James and John saw this, they said, "Lord, do you want us to command fire to come down from heaven and consume them, just as Elijah did?" But He turned and rebuked them. And said, "You do not know what manner of spirit you are of, for the Son of Man did not come to destroy men's lives but to save them." And they went to another village. Luke 9:54-56.

It is hard to imagine that they seemed to think it would be a good idea to call down fire from heaven and consume them. I believe Jesus was surprised at their overreaction. It is like Jesus said, "Seriously, you guys are so wrong." "That is not what I came to do." "I came to preach the gospel (good news) and save people, not destroy them."

Unfortunately, some Christians today still have a judgemental attitude if they are not received. There is nothing worse than being misunderstood or rejected. However, the

New Covenant is a covenant of grace, unlike Moses's old legalistic judgemental law.

Admit you made a mistake

Some Christians never want to admit they made a mistake or got it wrong. They are convinced they are always right and will justify themselves on different issues. It would be much easier to admit you made a mistake or said, "I'm sorry, but it seemed right at the time."

In their book *Mistakes Were Made (But Not by Me): Why We Justify Foolish Beliefs, Bad Decisions, and Hurtful Acts*, Carol Tavris and Elliot Aronson say, "Admitting we are wrong is difficult because it hurts our self-esteem, but the pain is temporary. Failing to admit we are wrong keeps us locked in bad decisions and behaviours." This book explores cognitive dissonance and how people convince themselves that their actions and beliefs are justified, even when wrong. It dives into self-justification and its consequences.

We can seem to have it right, convinced that the Holy Spirit is leading us, only to be wrong. Our selfish desires, wishes, and plans usually lead us astray when this happens.

So, I would suggest the word "seemed" can be positive in this context, that it is a perception that leaves room for human error when making some decisions. But this is no excuse for us to become slack when seeking guidance from the Holy Spirit.

Seems Like a Good Idea

Chapter 8

Believe in the goodness of God

How do we define a good idea? The word "good" is used in various ways depending on the context. It usually refers to something morally right, desirable, and beneficial.

So, considering the context of Acts 15:28. *"It seemed good to the Holy Spirit and to us."* We could say that their decision at the Jerusalem Council seemed morally right, desirable and beneficial.

If we refer to a good person, we refer to their character. If we refer to a good car, it would be its performance. If we referred to a good relationship, it would be friendship and loyalty.

Wikipedia says, "Good is that which is to be preferred and prescribed; not evil." (The opposite of evil). We need to bear this in mind when we refer to having faith in the goodness of God. We must believe that God is good all the time.

God does not just do good; He is good. His goodness can be defined as morally excellent, virtuous, just, and righteous.

John MacArthur says, "God's goodness is the perfect sum, source, and standard (for Himself and His creatures) of that which is wholesome (conducive to well-being), virtuous, beneficial, and beautiful."

It raises the question, "If God is so good, why does He allow evil to exist? This isn't easy to answer. God asks us to believe in His goodness despite the existence of evil. We could say evil only exists in the absence of God.

David believed in the goodness of God

David said, *"I would have lost heart unless I had believed that I would see the goodness of the Lord in the land of the living."* Psalm 27:13.

Why did David make this declaration?

In this context, David probably faced opposition and threats from his enemies. He also made some terrible mistakes and may have been reflecting on them. But despite the challenges, he had faith to see the goodness of God in his lifetime.

It is a verse we must embrace as Christians when we face various trials and reflect on our mistakes. Despite whatever evil intent is directed toward us, we must believe that God's goodness will enable us to overcome and survive.

David implies that he would have lost heart (or given up) unless he believed (had faith) that he would see (experience)

God's goodness in his lifetime.

He had already experienced God's goodness as a shepherd boy minding the sheep. To protect them, he was able to kill a bear and a lion with his bare hands. As a teenager, he slayed the giant Goliath. Then, he had to flee as a fugitive from the wrath of King Saul. Eventually, he was anointed as the King of Israel. He had every good reason to have faith in God's goodness.

The character and nature of God

The very character and nature of God reflect His goodness. *"Give thanks to the Lord, for He is good, His love endures forever."* Psalm 107:1.

God is loving, kind, merciful, just, and righteous. He is the complete package. There is no evil in Him. He only wants to do us good, for He knows what is best for us in this life.

In his book God is Good: He is Better than You Think, Bill Johnson says, "The goodness of God is foundational to trusting Him in difficult times. If I believe that God is good, I must believe He is always good."

Working together for our good

It is hard to believe everything works together for our good when going through trials that test our faith, but we must accept it.

"We know that all things work together for good to those who love God, to those who are the called according to His purpose." Romans 8:28.

This is a comfort for us as Christians. It does not mean that everything that happens is good. But God, in His infinite wisdom, can work all things out for our good. We may not see it at the time, but we usually look back and see how God made it all work out for our good.

I did not like the thought of a Bible College in Port Moresby. It had a high crime rate and was a dangerous place to live. A disused rubber plantation house and facilities I had visited on an earlier mission trip near the beginning of the famous Kokoda Trail became available to us. When I looked at it, I loved the location; it was quiet and peaceful, set in a mountainous jungle area. I think God used it to get me to PNG. But before we could finalise things, the PNG government requisitioned the plantation. So, we had no other option but to build the college dormitory on the existing church property in Port Moresby.

In retrospect, it all worked out for good. As lovely as it was on the plantation, it would not have been viable long-term. It was too far from the city for supplies, and there would have been issues with power and water. Port Moresby was by far the better option.

Jesus went about doing good

"How God anointed Jesus of Nazareth with the Holy Spirit and with power, who went about doing good and healing all who were oppressed of the devil, for God was with Him." Acts 10:38.

How did He do good? He healed all who the devil oppressed. Notice how it says, God was with Him." Yes, God is good and wants to do good.

Jesus was anointed with the Holy Spirit and with power. He was fulfilling His ministry, which He revealed the day He stood up in the synagogue and read from the book of Isaiah the prophet.

"The Spirit of the Lord is upon Me because He has anointed Me to preach the gospel to the poor; He has sent Me to heal the broken hearted, to proclaim liberty to the captives and recovery of sight to the blind, to set at liberty those who are oppressed." Luke 4:18.

The devil is evil and has bound people with sin, sickness, disease, and demonic oppression. The devil will always oppress people, which is a part of his wicked ways. But Jesus came to do people good by liberating them from the oppressor.

Jesus forgave sins and delivered people not only from the devil's oppression but also from the power of sin, death and hell. The goodness of God offers eternal life for all those who will believe.

The gospel means good news

Jesus came preaching the gospel of the kingdom of God and laid a foundation for the apostles and early church to follow. The word gospel can be translated from Greek as "good news" or "good message." In my book The Ambiguous Kingdom, I fully address this teaching.

People turn to Christ for many different reasons. Maybe

they fear judgment in tragedy or are convicted of their sins. Whatever the case, God's goodness leads us to repentance.

"Do you despise the riches of His goodness, forbearance, and longsuffering, not knowing that the goodness of God leads you to repentance.? Romans 2:4.

No matter what you have done (I have done things I am ashamed of), you can still repent and turn to Christ. This is the grace and love of God shown to us when we do not deserve it. It is the gift of salvation by the grace of God. You can turn to Christ now if you come in faith and declare Him your Saviour and Lord.

This is the good news that will be preached all over the world before the return of Christ.

"And this gospel of the kingdom will be preached in all the world as a witness to all nations, and then the end will come." Matthew 24:14.

Expect good outcomes in future

Do you expect a promising future for your life? David, Jesus, the apostles, and the early church all expected good outcomes for the future.

The decision the council at Jerusalem in Acts 15 had made concerning the Gentiles coming to faith in Christ was put in a letter and sent back to Antioch, where they were having trouble. What was the outcome of this letter? Was it good?

"They came to Antioch, and when they gathered the multitude together, they delivered the letter. When they had read it, they rejoiced over its

encouragement." Acts 15: 30-31.

They rejoiced over its encouragement. It was a good outcome. They were happy because it gave clear direction for resolving the problem.

Seems Like a Good Idea

Chapter 9
Walking the road less travelled

Sometimes, we need to walk the road less travelled. This may mean choosing an unconventional path that we have not taken before—something outside our comfort zone, a little riskier, and adventurous. Good ideas are usually innovative, which means there is always an element of risk attached to them.

The last time we drove from the Gold Coast to Melbourne, I wanted to avoid driving through Sydney traffic, so I turned off before we got to Sydney to take what I thought would be a shortcut. It may have been the road less travelled and not so much traffic, but it was narrow, full of hills and bends. It was an adventure but cost us an extra day's travel.

In a way, when Jesus and the early church preached the gospel, they challenged people under the law to walk the road less travelled. They presented a road of grace and faith in Christ under an unfamiliar new covenant.

In Acts 15, the council at Jerusalem made a decision that

compelled Jewish and Gentile Christians to take the road less travelled, the road of grace. Sometimes, we need to do the same.

In his book, *The Road Less Travelled*, M. Scott Peck says, "The truth is that our finest moments are most likely to occur when we feel deeply uncomfortable, unhappy, or unfulfilled. Only in such moments, propelled by our discomfort, will we likely step out of our ruts and start searching for different ways or truer answers."

Taste and see that the Lord is good

God invites us to taste and see that He is good. The emphasis is on testing Him to see if it is true. It is an invitation to experience His goodness to know if He can be trusted.

"O taste and see that the Lord is good; Blessed is the man that trusts in Him." Psalm 34.

When we preach the gospel, we ask people to turn to Christ and experience God's goodness. It is a metaphor, much like tasting food to see if it is tasty and good for eating.

Recently, my wife had an ankle bone fusion as a result of a broken leg many years ago. While she was recovering, for a couple of months, she was not allowed to weight bear, so I had to do all the cooking (a road less travelled for me).

I would taste the food before serving it to ensure it was good enough to eat. It was a steep learning curve, and despite a few flops, we have survived. She now tells me I am so good a cook that she wants me to keep going. What does the Bible say about flattery?

God may be on the road less travelled

God likes to surprise us, walk the road less travelled, and do new things.

> *"Behold, I will do a new thing; now it shall spring forth; shall you not know it? I will even make a road in the wilderness and rivers in the desert."* Isaiah 43:19.

When God does something new, the desert begins to bloom; God can make something out of nothing. He can make what seems to be barren become fruitful and plentiful. He can do the same in your life.

We took the road less travelled when we went to PNG to start a Bible College. We left a secure home and ministry, uprooted ourselves as a family, and went to a foreign country to start something we had never done before. All we had was a new idea that became a vision born of the Holy Spirit.

While in a coffee shop the other day, my wife picked up a magazine called "New Idea." It caught my attention; even though it has been around for years in Australia, I had never bothered to check it out. I looked it up online and discovered "New Idea" was originally an Australian magazine founded in 1902 by James Norton. As its name reflects, it is to inspire new ideas. It originally intended to appeal to women and give them new ideas and suggestions for cooking, healthier lifestyles, dressing for an occasion, family activities, and engaging with society. It was full of new ideas and was a fitting name for such a creative magazine.

Peter walks the road less travelled

Jesus had sent the disciples off in a boat without Him to cross the Sea of Galilee while He stayed on land to pray.

They were caught in a storm in the early morning hours. Jesus appeared, walking on the water toward them. Peter accepted Jesus' invitation to leave the boat and come to Him walking on water. Peter stepped out of the boat onto the road less travelled and walked on the water.

"But immediately Jesus spoke to them, saying, "Be of good cheer! It is I; do not be afraid." And Peter answered Him and said, "Lord, if it is You, command me to come to You on the water." So, He said, "Come." And when Peter had come down out of the boat, he walked on the water to go to Jesus." Matthew 14:27-29.

Peter needed only one word, "Come." He did not hesitate to accept the invitation. When the Lord invites us to take the road less travelled, are we willing to step out in faith like Peter?

However, when Peter saw how windy it was, he was afraid and began to sink, as did his faith.

"But when he saw that the wind was boisterous, he was afraid; and beginning to sink, he cried out saying, "Lord, save me." Immediately, Jesus stretched out His hand and caught him." Matthew 14:30.

Peter miraculously walked on water, but the moment he took his eyes off Jesus, he was in trouble. Does that sound familiar to you?

Exploring roads less travelled

This applies to both natural and spiritual roads less travelled. I love the outdoors and have always enjoyed exploring.

Some years ago, I decided to climb Mount Warning in northern NSW. Although there was a rough walking track and a rope handrail to pull yourself up near the top, it was exhausting. But the view was worth it once you reached the summit. I found it was just as hard going down again. I remember how sore I was and how long it took me to recover. I had to rest for days.

Before I was married, one of my first jobs was working shifts on a newspaper, which meant we often had a day off during the week. So, I would like to wander off on my own and explore the nearby Grampian Mountain Range. I would drive along roads less travelled into the mountains and then walk through the rugged bush exploring.

I loved the bush and the wildlife, with the potential to see all kinds of birds, kangaroos, emus, wallabies, koalas, snakes, goannas, echidnas, and fish in lovely refreshing streams.

One day, I stumbled across an old, overgrown mining area where, long ago, people had been digging for gold. There were several mine shafts and tunnels to explore. I found no gold, but I discovered plenty of quartz crystals. It became my secret place for years. You never know what you will find on the road less travelled.

I recently heard an interview with Sir Bob Geldof, an Irish singer, songwriter, and activist who said if he had the choice between a gig that would be worth big dollars to him and a gig on the road less travelled, he would choose the road less travelled every time. Why? Because he would find it more adventurous, stimulating, exciting, and challenging.

An invitation for weary travellers

We face spiritual pressures in the ministry. I was fortunate enough to have good secretaries, although there was one who could not understand why I was not in the office every day of the week. I would spend one day a week at home studying, praying, and spiritually refreshing myself to prepare for ministry.

Some people do not realise how demanding and draining ministry can be if we do not keep ourselves topped up. Jesus was aware of this and sometimes drew aside with His disciples to pray and rest.

You may feel you have been travelling the road less travelled for a long time, encountering the storms of life, and have become weary and worn out. You may desperately need to rest.

Today, Jesus extends to you a fabulous invitation.

"Come to Me all you that labour and are heavily laden, and I will give you rest. Take My yoke upon you and learn from Me, for I am gentle and lowly in heart, and you will find rest for your souls." Matthew 11: 28-29.

If this applies to you, I encourage you to accept this invitation because you are weary from travelling the road less travelled. Set aside time, relax and rest in the presence of the Lord.

Seems Like a Good Idea

Chapter 10

Spiritual and natural discernment

Christians need both spiritual and natural discernment. What do I mean by that? Although we touch on this briefly in other chapters, it is worth expounding further.

Discernment has many facets to it. It is the process of making informed judgments in complex situations. It involves evaluating and assessing various factors that help us make wise decisions.

We naturally discern who we should align with by observing and understanding values and morals and developing healthy relationships. This may be effective when choosing a partner or a career path that fits our calling and purpose. We will also need discernment in the home and the workplace regarding potential scams that can destroy our ethics, vision, and future.

In Acts 15:28, the council at Jerusalem arrived at its informed judgment because it discerned the situation regarding certain

Jewish Christians demanding that the Gentiles coming to faith in Christ be circumcised according to Jewish customs and law. They were discerning both the spiritual and natural issues. Then, after much discussion, prayer, and wisdom, they could make their final decision.

Discerning the signs of the times

When the Pharisees and Sadducees came and asked Jesus for a sign from heaven to authenticate His authority as to who He was, He said to them,

> *"When it is evening, you say, "It will be fair weather, for the sky is red, and in the morning, "It will be foul weather today, for the sky is red and threatening." Hypocrites! You know how to discern the face of the sky, but you cannot discern the signs of the times."* Matthew 16:1-3.

So, Jesus draws a parallel using natural and spiritual discernment to illustrate a point. He is saying you can discern the weather, but you cannot discern the signs of the times. We all have sure signs we look for when trying to discern the weather, probably depending on our location. As a boy, I remember my dad pointing to the clouds and telling me the signs concerning the weather being good, nasty, hot, wet, or windy. This became very helpful later in life.

Yes, we do need to discern the signs of the times today. When I consider what is happening in and around Israel at the time of writing, we may see Bible prophecy unfolding in our day and age. But this is straying from our subject.

However, in this context, I think Jesus refers to more than

just the signs leading up to His second coming. He refers to the fact that He has come as the Messiah, yet they do not understand how He could be the Messiah.

The sign of Jonah

Jesus assures them that no sign except the sign of Jonah shall be given.

"A wicked and adulterous generation seeks after a sign, and no sign shall be given to it except the sign of the prophet Jonah." Matthew 16:4.

He refers to the story of Jonah, a prophet who was swallowed by a great fish and spent three days and three nights in its belly before being spat out alive. This is prophetic of Jesus' death and resurrection, as to how He was to spend three days in the tomb before His resurrection.

So, Jesus is telling them that this is the only miraculous sign they will receive; it will be the ultimate proof of His divine mission to authenticate that He is who claims to be the Son of God, the Messiah.

Moral Discernment

Jesus said, *"A wicked and adulterous generation seeks after a sign."* He describes His generation from a moral point of view. It is only reasonable for Jesus to expect us to have moral discernment in our generation.

It is the ability to discern what is good, just, and proper. It is not so much us judging others as assessing what is right and wrong. It is then up to us to make wise decisions based on that discernment.

Today, we face so many complex moral issues, such as same-sex partners, adultery, fornication, and all kinds of immoral and deceptive practices.

From a Christian perspective, we are meant to make wise choices that would please the Lord. To help us do that, we have been given the ability to discern spirits.

In PNG, I depended on discerning evil spirits and the deliverance ministry. The spirit world was interwoven into their culture. Although this is a valuable and necessary gift, there are other aspects to discerning spirits.

Three aspects to discerning spirits

One of the gifts of the Holy Spirit is "Discerning of spirits", as listed in 1 Corinthians 12:10. I think this can manifest itself in different ways.

1. **Discerning evil spirits -**

    Several incidents are recorded in the Bible where Jesus and the Apostles discerned evil spirits.

    The disciples had been trying to cast out a spirit from a deaf and mute boy but could not, so they brought him to Jesus. He rebuked the unclean spirit (all evil spirits are unclean), named it, and commanded it to come out.

"He rebuked the unclean spirit, saying to it: "Deaf and dumb spirit, I command you come out of him and enter him no more!" Then the spirit cried out, convulsed him greatly, and came out of him." Mark 9:25-26.

I remember praying for an unsaved man who was destroying his marriage because of his riotous drunken behaviour. I led him to the Lord in prayer, then said to him, "Spirit of alcohol, come out of this man." He was thrown across the floor dry reaching, then got up, shook his head, and said, "What just happened? I feel great."

He became a dedicated Christian with his wife and family and started attending our church regularly.

In the Bible, there was a girl possessed with a spirit of divination who made her master much profit by fortune-telling. She followed Paul for many days, shouting out accolades, but Paul was not impressed by her flattery.

"This girl followed Paul and us and cried out, saying, "These men are the servants of the Most-High, God, who proclaim to us the way of salvation." Paul, greatly annoyed, turned and said to the spirit, "I command you in the name of Jesus Christ to come out of her." And he came out that very hour." Acts 16:16-18.

Paul discerned that her flattery was the mocking

work of a spirit of divination

2. Discerning the thoughts of a person -

Several incidents are recorded in the Bible where a person's spirit is discerned.

When they brought the paralytic man to Jesus for healing, He said to the man, *"Your sins are forgiven you."* But the scribes said, *"Who can forgive sins but God alone?"*

"But immediately Jesus perceived in His spirit that they reasoned thus within themselves, He said to them, "Why do you reason about these things in your hearts?" Mark 2:7-8

Jesus discerned in His spirit what they were reasoning in their hearts. This was not guesswork; He knew what they were thinking by the gift of discernment.

How many times have you been talking to someone and discerned their thinking?

3. Discerning faith in a person -

Paul was in Lystra, and there was a man who had a disability and had never walked. He was listening to Paul preaching.

"This man heard Paul speaking; Paul, observing

him intently and seeing that he had faith to be healed, said loudly, "Stand up straight on your feet!" And he leapt and walked. Acts 14:8-9.

Paul discerned he had faith to be healed. Have you ever prayed for someone and felt, in your heart, that they had faith to be healed or faith for whatever they desired?

So, spiritual and natural discernment are great tools in our lives. They are the work of the Holy Spirit.

Jim Hart's The Gift of Discernment: How to Make Wise Decisions is excellent teaching. He defines discernment as recognising and evaluating spiritual influences, helping believers differentiate between God's truth and deceptive teachings. He stresses the necessity of testing all teachings against scripture, as false teaching can often appear convincing but ultimately can lead believers astray. He urges that cultivating discernment is crucial for spiritual maturity. It enables believers to grow in their faith by understanding and responding more effectively to God's guidance.

So, when your next idea seems good and inspired by the Holy Spirit, you may find the gift of discernment helpful in evaluating its authenticity and practical application.

Seems Like a Good Idea

Chapter 11

Is God approachable and flexible?

When we implement an idea that seems good, and things do not go according to plan, is there scope to change our approach, or are we locked in because we think the idea is from God? This opens a Pandora's box and leads to questions like, "Is God approachable and flexible?"

After all, if we consider the holiness and majesty of God and that He dwells in unapproachable light, it gives us the impression that no one can stand in His presence, lest they be consumed.

"Who alone has immortality, dwelling in unapproachable light, whom no man has seen or can see to whom be honour and everlasting power. Amen." 1 Timothy 6:16.

God is also portrayed as immutable, unchanging, and perfect. *"For I am the Lord, I do not change."* Malachi 3:6.

Therefore, if God is perfect, He does not need to change, adapt, or be flexible. Why should He consider human desires and requests? Yes, there is one reason: He is relational.

God is relatable

In the book *God: A Biography* by Jack Miles, he says, "The profound originality of a divine-human pact in which both parties complain endlessly about each other has too rarely been acknowledged as such." God's character's approachable and flexible side becomes the book's central theme. He explores how God evolves, especially in His interactions with humanity. God anticipates human responses, which leads Him to react with more remarkable restraint, allowing events to unfold without interfering. He shows how God shows flexibility not just in terms of power but also in relationships.

Because God is relational, and while His character and nature may never change, He has created us in His image to be sons and daughters and a part of His family.

Despite our puny weaknesses, compared to God, He desires to relate to us in our human form. Therefore, this makes God approachable.

I have known some pastors to be more interested in their ministry and image than in relating to people.

I remember picking up a visiting minister from the airport who wanted me to stop at his father's house to see his dad, who was a high-profile minister. I was looking forward to meeting him.

But when we arrived at the house, he said, "You stay here in the car. My dad will not be interested in meeting you; he is not good with people he does not know." I was embarrassed to think somebody in ministry was not good at meeting new people. Well, God is not like that!

Approachable through prayer

From a Christian perspective, we have what seems to be a contradiction when considering the grace and mercy of God according to the gospel. Because of Jesus, we are invited to relate to God through prayer.

"For we do not have a High Priest who cannot sympathise with our weaknesses, but was in all points tempted as we are, yet without sin. Let us therefore come boldly to the throne of grace, that we may obtain mercy and find grace to help in time of need." Hebrews 4:16.

God understands our weaknesses and is willing to help us. He now invites us to approach his throne of grace to obtain mercy and find grace to help us in our time of need.

The implication is that God is approachable through prayer at any time, place, or for any need we may have. The invitation is to come boldly to the throne of grace.

We are not coming to a throne of judgment to meet with an austere, unapproachable God who is unconcerned about our needs.

Maybe you think you are not worthy to approach God in prayer. That is a lie from the pit of hell. God sees you through the blood of Christ. He has forgiven you, making you acceptable in His beloved.

"He made us accepted in the beloved. In Him we have redemption through His blood, the forgiveness of sins, according to the riches of His grace." Ephesians 1:6-7.

I expound this truth in detail in my book But for the Grace of God Go I. This is why we are told to come boldly (with confidence) to the throne of grace.

God will never reject you, cast you out, or disown you. Jesus said, *"All that the Father gives Me will come to Me, and the one who comes to Me I will by no means cast out."* John 6:37.

Anyone can approach God. It does not matter your nationality, background, or whatever you have done; you are invited to come boldly to the throne of grace. God will not reject anyone with a repentant heart to seek forgiveness.

In Acts 15:28, they were debating whether the Gentiles should be accepted without being circumcised. However, the scripture is clear on this subject.

"For there is no distinction between Jew and Greek, for the same Lord over all is rich to all who call upon Him. For whoever calls on the name of the Lord shall be saved." Romans 10:12-13.

How flexible is God?

We have seen that God is approachable. But it raises the question, "How flexible is He when we approach Him?

If we have a relationship with God through prayer, can we negotiate with Him? Can we plead with Him in the hope that He might change His mind?

This may depend upon your theology as to your view on His flexibility. But there are Biblical instances where He works through human choices and circumstances to establish His will, even if the choices seem contrary to His original intentions.

Biblical examples of His flexibility

Moses -

God was angry with Israel and said to Moses, *"Leave Me alone, that My wrath may burn hot against them and I may consume them. And I will make of you a great nation." Then Moses pleaded with the Lord.* Exodus 32:10-11.

Moses bought a whole lot of reasons as to why the Lord should not consume them. They were God's people whom He had delivered from the bondage of the Egyptians. Now, you are going to kill them. What would the Egyptians think about that? The Lord listened to Moses and changed his mind.

"So, the Lord relented from the harm He said He would do to His people." Exodus 32:14.

Hezekiah -

Hezekiah was sick and near death. God sent Isaiah the prophet to him, and he said to him,

"Set your house in order, for you shall die and not live." Isaiah 38:1.

When Hezekiah heard it, he pleaded with the Lord, reminding Him of how he had served Him faithfully and was loyal to his calling. Hezekiah wept bitterly before the Lord.

When God heard this and saw his reaction, He was flexible enough to change his decision.

"And the word came to Isaiah, saying, "Go and tell Hezekiah, "Thus says the Lord, the God of David your father: "I have heard your prayer, I have seen your tears; surely I will add to your life fifteen years." Isaiah 38:5.

Jonah -

God sent Jonah to Nineveh to warn the Ninevites that God would destroy the city in forty days. They listened to Jonah, repented, and turned to God.

"Then God saw their works, that they turned from their evil way; and God relented from the disaster that He said He would bring upon them, and He did not do it." Jonah 3:10.

So, God was flexible enough to change His mind when He saw how they repented. There was only one person who was not happy - Jonah.

"But it displeased Jonah exceedingly, and he became angry. So, he prayed to the Lord and said, "Ah, Lord, was not this what I said when I was still in my country? Therefore, I fled previously to Tarshish; for I know that you are a gracious and merciful God,

slow to anger and abundant in lovingkindness; One who relents from doing harm. Therefore now, O Lord, please take my life from me, for it is better for me to die than to live!" Jonah 4:1-3.

Jonah was angry and upset. He was embarrassed because he had preached that God would destroy the city, but it did not happen. He was so humiliated that he wanted to die.

But God pointed out to Jonah that he had a problem with his attitude. Jonah was more concerned about a plant giving him shade dying than he was about the city of Nineveh, with its one hundred and twenty thousand people perishing together with their livestock.

State your case

If God is approachable and flexible, it leaves room for us to negotiate and "state our case." What does that mean? There is no guarantee that He will change His mind. It is a phrase that God uses to challenge people to explain (state their case) because of their ungodly behaviour. He is giving them a chance to justify themselves.

"I, even I, am He who blots out your transgression for My own sake, and I will not remember your sins. Put Me in remembrance; let us contend together; State your case, that you may be acquitted". Isaiah 43:25-26.

God is revealing His flexibility. He invites Israel to put Him in remembrance of His forgiveness, let us contend together, and state your case. I am willing to listen, and maybe I will acquit you.

What about you? Do you need to state your case before the Lord?

Chapter 12

The ripple effect of a good idea

We are all familiar with the "ripple effect", which occurs when a single action or event spreads like ripples on water when a stone is dropped into it.

A ripple effect happens when a good idea results in an invention or discovery. It may begin in a scientific lab and then spread around the world. For example, penicillin was one of the most significant discoveries in medical history for treating infections. It has become one of the most effective antibiotics, saving millions of lives.

Breakthroughs, like discovering penicillin, inspire others to experiment and develop creative ideas in medicine and technology that can change the world.

One significant innovation can create another, leading to a cycle of progressive events.

In his book *The Butterfly Effect: How Your Life Matters,* Andy Andrews says, "Every single thing you do matters. You have been created as one of a kind. You have been created in order to make a difference. You have within you the power to change the world." He emphasises the idea that we all have the ability to create a ripple effect with profound consequences.

It only takes one important decision

It only takes one crucial decision to set a ripple effect in motion. The decision of the Jerusalem Council in Acts 15 had a ripple effect that changed the course of History. What happened as a result?

1. Unity for Christians -

It enabled the Gentiles coming to faith in Christ to join the early church without causing division. It helped to maintain the unity of the Spirit.

2. Christianity beyond Judaism –

It helped to spread the gospel to a non-Jewish world, allowing rapid growth of Christianity throughout the Roman Empire.

3. Theological and cultural changes –

There was no longer a need to adhere to the Mosaic law. Understanding grace and faith in Christ made radical theological and cultural changes.

4. Opened the way for missionary work –

It made it easier to spread the gospel. Gentiles could follow Christ without considering Jewish customs. This decision was a great help to Paul as he embarked on missionary journeys, planting churches across Asia Minor, Greece and beyond.

5. Gentiles influence Christianity –

Over time, Christianity drifted away from Jewish traditions and customs as more Gentiles joined the Christian faith. This influenced the rapid spread of the gospel and Christianity as we know it today.

The ripple effect of our decisions

When I came to faith in Christ, my decision to become a Christian had a profound "ripple effect" on my life and many others.

As far back as I can remember, I believed in God and desired to know Him. I did not have a regular church background apart from attending a Presbyterian Sunday School.

I had met a pastor in my secular job who was pioneering a Charismatic Church in a house in my hometown, Horsham, Victoria. He sensed I was searching and kept inviting me to one of his meetings.

I finally accepted his invitation. It was a hot summer night, and when the pastor gave an altar call, I broke out in a cold sweat, but I managed to work up enough courage to go forward and commit my life to Christ.

That decision had a "ripple effect" on my family, friends, and future. My lifestyle completely changed. Many of my friends and family were bewildered and unable to understand what had happened to me.

But those praying for me were overjoyed (the pastor had people praying for me). As a young, born-again Christian, I wanted to serve God and train for ministry. Around that time, I met my dream girl, Caroline, and we married and headed for Bible College.

I ended up in full-time ministry as a pastor and missionary for over forty years, leading many to Christ and helping them grow as Christians. I saw many lives changed in miraculous ways.

That one decision I made in that humble, seemingly insignificant house meeting has resulted in an incredible "ripple effect" that has impacted my family, friends, and many other lives for Christ.

Sometimes, people tell me the story about how I ministered to them. Most of the time, I forget until they start sharing. Then, they explain the incredible ripple effect that had on others.

The "ripple effect" of Christianity

The ripple effect of Christianity was a turning point in history that shaped and changed the world.

We have already discussed the ripple effect of Acts 15's

decision to accept the Gentiles through grace and faith in Christ without requiring them to conform to Jewish laws and traditions.

The most outstanding and noticeable ripple effect in the Bible and upon history is the life, ministry, death and resurrection of Jesus. He redeemed us from the curse of sin and death upon the human race. Jesus and His followers became known as Christians, who turned the world upside down. (Acts 17:6).

Saul, who became Paul, had a dramatic conversion that had a profound ripple effect on Christianity.

"Saul, Saul, "Why are you persecuting Me?" And He said, "Who are you, Lord?" "I am Jesus, whom you are persecuting."... So, he, trembling and astonished, said, "Lord, what do You want me to do?" Acts 9:4-6.

A bright light blinded him. So, the Lord sent Ananias to lay hands on him to open his eyes. But Ananias was hesitant because he had heard about Saul persecuting Christians in Jerusalem.

"But the Lord said to him, "Go for he is a chosen vessel of mine to bear My name before Gentiles, kings, and the children of Israel." Acts 9:15.

When Paul stood before King Agrippa, he said, *"I was not disobedient to the heavenly vision."* Acts 26: 19.

Thank God Paul was obedient to his calling. His conversion and letters have been invaluable in shaping Christianity and establishing sound doctrine for the church.

What about you?

Seems Like a Good Idea

Maybe your life has already had a ripple effect. If not, there is always time. Your good ideas inspired by the Holy Spirit and the decisions you make today may also have a profound ripple effect on humanity for generations to come.

Chapter 13

Do you desire more of God?

What do I mean by asking, "Do you desire more of God?" Is it possible to have more of God? More than you already have?

It does not mean God is fragmented or in pieces to be rationed to us. After being Christians for some time, we can become comfortable and complacent, thinking we know all there is to know about God and Christianity.

The danger is that we become rigid and dogmatic about what we believe and defenders of the faith as we know it. We can become reluctant to explore more of God and investigate different viewpoints and new ideas. We can stop hearing the voice of the Holy Spirit, become stuck in past revelations of God, and not be open to what God is saying and doing today. When this happens, the fire within us begins to die, and we can become lukewarm.

We can become set in our ways and no longer willing to rise to the challenge of new ideas, and sometimes, our hearts are hardened to the leading of the Holy Spirit.

Do not let the fire die within

You may feel fully committed already and do not have time to become more involved in the church's life. That is fine, and I understand that.

I am not necessarily talking about doing more to desire more of God. I am referring to your heart attitude concerning your relationship with God.

We must be careful not to lose our compassion and hunger for more of God. Jesus cautioned the church at Ephesus because they had left their first love (Revelation 2:4) and the church at Laodicea for becoming lukewarm (Revelation 3:16).

Although this is written for churches and is something church leaders need to address, I'm sure we can also apply it to us as individuals.

In his book, *The Pursuit of God*, A. W. Tozer says, "We are called to an everlasting preoccupation of God. To have found God and still pursue Him is life."

Throughout history, including those in the Bible, many men and women have been known for their deep hunger and thirst for more of God.

Those who gathered at the Jerusalem Council (Acts 15) desired more of an understanding of God doctrinally by coming together to discuss, pray, and sort out the issue at hand to decide to resolve the problem they were facing.

The example of Apollos

Apollos is introduced as a Jew from Alexandria who arrives at Ephesus. He is described as being -

"An eloquent man, mighty in the scriptures, instructed in the way of the Lord, fervent in spirit, he spoke and taught accurately the things of the Lord, though he knew only the baptism of John." Acts 18:24-25.

Apollos had a great ministry. He was well-educated, knew the scriptures, was a great speaker, and was influential. What more could you want? He seemed to have it all. But he was still open for more.

"He began to speak boldly in the synagogue. When Aquila and Priscilla heard him, they took him aside and explained to him the way of God more accurately." Acts 18:26.

Apollos knew the way of Christ but was limited in his understanding of the gospel because he only knew of John's baptism. So, Aquila and Priscilla took him aside to explain the way of God more accurately.

He could have said, "I know enough," "Who do you think you are to instruct me?" But he didn't; he was hungry for more of God. His attitude was probably, "Bring it on, please tell me more". They must have explained the grace of God, Christian baptism, which identifies with Jesus' death, burial, and resurrection, and the baptism in the Holy Spirit.

We do not have clarification on what happened, but Apollos went on to preach at Corinth.

"When he arrived, he greatly helped those who had believed through grace; for he vigorously refuted the Jews publicly, showing them the scriptures that Jesus is the Christ." Acts 18:27-28.

Apollos understood the gospel after his time with Aquila and Priscilla. Still, there is no specific reference to him being baptised in water or receiving the baptism in the Holy Spirit. But one would assume he did after speaking with Aquila and Priscilla.

Disciples open to more of God

Interestingly, when Paul came to Ephesus, where Apollos had been, he asked some disciples -

"Did you receive the Holy Spirit when you believed?" So, they said to him, "We have not so much as heard whether there is a Holy Spirit." And He said to them, "Into what then were you baptised?" So, they said, into John's baptism." Acts 19:2-3.

We don't know if it was the same group of believers that Apollos ministered to. But like Apollos, they only knew of John's baptism.

Paul explained the need for Christian baptism, and we assume the Baptism in the Holy Spirit, seeing this as his leading question, "Did you receive the Holy Spirit when you believed?"

"When they heard this, they were baptised in the name of the Lord Jesus. And when Paul laid hands on them, the Holy Spirit came upon them, and they spoke with tongues and prophesied." Acts 19:5-6.

So, they were baptised in water and the Holy Spirit, just like on the day of Pentecost.

Hungry for more of God

When I first came to faith in Christ, I was hungry for God. I could not get enough of Him. My life had dramatically changed. I wanted to serve God in ministry. I devoured books, listened to tapes, attended conferences, and annoyed the pastor by asking many hard-to-answer questions. He finally suggested that I enrol in Bible College.

When I heard teachings on the baptism in the Holy Spirit and how it would empower you for service and the benefits of speaking in tongues - how when you speak in tongues, you talk to God, you speak mysteries in the spirit, edify yourself, I thought, "Count me in, I need all the help I can get."

I wanted as much of God as possible to help me as a Christian and a potential ministry. So, I was baptised in the Holy Spirit and spoke in tongues; it has been an incredible blessing and help.

I first spoke in tongues at a prayer meeting. However, I had been told that the pattern was to be baptised in water first, so I tried to restrain myself until I was baptised in water, so I came up out of the water, speaking in tongues.

If you desire more of God, I would encourage you to seek to be baptised in the Holy Spirit if you have not done so already.

However, this does not mean you have arrived, and there is no need to desire more of God because you have it all. There is always more!

Years ago, there was an ad on TV in which they would offer a special deal on some item and then throw in a few extras, each time saying, "There is still more," to make you think you were getting a bargain because of the extras.

I am not suggesting that God is doing that, but I share this to encourage you to pursue God with all your heart. There is always more!

God is unfathomable and eternal; there is no end to the mysteries He may have for you. Maintain that hunger for more of God, and they will be revealed to you by the Spirit.

"But as it is written: "Eye has not seen, nor ear heard, nor entered into the heart of man the things which God has prepared for those who love Him." "But God has revealed them to us through His Spirit. For the Spirit searches all things, yes, the deep things of God." 1 Corinthians 2:9-10.

Others who desired more of God

There are many other examples in the Bible of those wanting more of God. Of course, we have all the disciples of Jesus except Judas, who betrayed Him.

We could elaborate on them all, but I will briefly share a few prominent ones from the Bible.

Moses –

He sought a deeper intimacy with God and prayed, *"Now show me your glory."* Exodus 33:18.

David –

He longed for more of God; he wrote, *"As the deer pants for streams of water, so my soul pants for you, my God."* Psalm 42:1.

Mary of Bethany –

We assume Mary was hungry for more of God. She was the sister of Martha and Lazarus. She chose to sit at Jesus' feet to hear His word. Martha wanted her to help serve, but Jesus said what she had chosen to do was a good thing. (Luke 10:39-42).

The apostle Paul –

Paul expressed his desire to know God more deeply.

"That I might know Him and the power of His resurrection, and the fellowship of His sufferings, being conformed to His death. If by any means I might attain to the resurrection from the dead. Not that I have already attained, or am already perfected; but I press on, that I might lay hold of that for which Christ Jesus has also laid hold of me." Philippians 3:10-12.

I love the way Paul says, "Not that I have already attained, or am already perfected." He implies that he still needs to mature and that there is still more to know about God. So, he will continue to press on to develop his relationship with God.

Are you open to more of God?

We can all learn from Paul's example.

Seems Like a Good Idea

Are you pressing on? Are you hungry for more of God? Do you know why He has called you? If you are willing to press on, you will discover more about God and yourself.

Chapter 14

Cast not away your confidence

"Therefore, do not cast away your confidence, which has great reward. For you have need of endurance, so that after you have done the will of God, you may receive the promise." Hebrews 10:35-36.

This is written in the context of "The just shall live by faith." So, whatever we may be going through in life, we should never lose our confidence.

Does this mean confidence in God or ourselves?

When you read the context in Hebrews, I believe it is both, but it primarily speaks of confidence in God. It refers to boldness and an assurance that God will not forsake or abandon you; cling to His promises despite persecution and opposition. It mentions the need for endurance as you walk in God's will. So, the bottom line is to remain confident despite whatever hardships you may be facing.

God imparts confidence to Joshua

After the death of Moses, his assistant Joshua was called by God to lead the people into the promised land. Joshua needed confidence to enter the land, drive out their enemies, and possess it.

God imparted confidence to him by encouraging Joshua with His word, promising to be with him and never to leave or forsake him.

"As I was with Moses, so I will be with you; I will never leave or forsake you. Be strong and of good courage"......"Do not be afraid or dismayed, for the Lord your God is with you wherever you go." Joshua 1:5-9.

This was a new challenge for Joshua and the people. Before they crossed the Jordan River to enter the promised land, Joshua encouraged the people with the word of the Lord. The officers also urged the people to follow the ark across the river, saying, *"For we have not passed this way before."* Joshua 3:4. This was to be a new experience.

We will all face challenges when we have not passed this way before. You may have a good idea inspired by the Holy Spirit. Are you up to the challenge? Are you prepared to step out in faith because you are confident that God is with you? Whatever you do, do not cast away your confidence and turn back, but move forward in faith.

A definition of confidence by Wikipedia

"Confidence is the feeling of belief or trust that a person or thing is reliable." (This would apply to God). "Self-confidence is trust in oneself. It involves a positive belief that one can generally accomplish what one wishes to do in the future. Self-confidence is not the same as self-esteem, which evaluates one's worth. Self-confidence is related to self-efficacy – belief in one's ability to accomplish a specific task or goal."

I would suggest that confidence in God also gives us the confidence in ourselves to survive and fulfil whatever God has called us to accomplish in life.

In his *Principles of Psychology*, the philosopher William James wrote, "Believe what is in the line of your needs, for only by such belief is the need fulfilled. Have faith that you can successfully make it, and your feet are nerved to its accomplishment." Another way of interpreting this would be to; "Put feet to your faith" by going into action.

Confidence to move forward in faith

God wants us to move forward in confidence. *"Now the just shall live by faith, but if anyone draws back, My soul has no pleasure in him."* Hebrews 10:38.

One thing God does not want us to do is to cast away our confidence and turn back (or backslide). He would rather we take a risk and move forward in faith because our confidence is in Him.

Confidence is like a propeller on a boat. It propels us forward in God. From a Christian perspective, our confidence is based on our positive belief system in the word of God and our outlook on life. It develops and grows with our faith.

I play golf and know how important it is to play that first hole well. Starting with a par or birdie will encourage you and boost your confidence for the rest of your game.

In a series of messages titled "I'm okay, and I'm on my way: Moving forward with confidence that God is on your side," Joyce Meyer says, "I may not be where I need to be, but thank God I am not where I used to be, I'm okay I'm on my way." We are already on our way and can all move forward confidently because God is on our side.

Confidence is catchy

We can gain confidence through the word of God and through others who have confidence in God. Confidence is catchy; it gains momentum as we move forward, and it will rub off on others.

You can sense or feel it when you talk to people. You may have complete confidence in some people but none in others. There have been times when we have been shopping for a particular item and find we have no confidence in the salesperson. They appear inexperienced and uncertain, lack knowledge, and have little confidence in their product. When this happens, we usually seek to talk to someone with more experience.

However, the other extreme is to be overconfident, arrogant, and proud. When this happens, we can make irrational or outlandish decisions that can be unreasonable and get us into trouble.

We were helping an elderly pastor struggling to maintain a

church of about thirty people. He would sometimes stand up and rave about his vision for a church of ten thousand people. We would all stare at him like stunned mullets. I could not help but think of the line from the Australian movie The Castle, "You must be dreaming." We did not share his enthusiasm and felt it was time to move on, but the church stayed the same. He was irrational, and his vision was out of his depth; it was too extreme to be realistic.

Confidence is an inner calm that God is in control. It gives us inner peace and security, for we know it is based on God's grace and our relationship with Him. We are to trust Him with all of our hearts.

Confidence to make decisions

Acts 15:28 confirms how the early church leaders came together confidently to discern God's will to defuse a potential ongoing problem. After seeking God's will, they had the confidence to make a decision, write a letter, send it off to those concerned, and follow it up. It was written confidently, delivered confidently, and received with confidence.

"The apostles. The elders, and the brethren, To the brethren who are of the Gentiles in Antioch, Syria, and Cilicia: Greetings. (followed by the contents of the letter)….. "So, when they were sent off, they came to Antioch, and when they had gathered the multitude together, they delivered the letter. When they had read it, they rejoiced over its encouragement." Acts 15:23-31.

Confidence ignites faith. Because of our confidence and faith, we will be significantly rewarded (here and now with spiritual strength and peace) and in eternity with rewards in heaven.

Confidence, like faith, will be tested

Joseph was sold into slavery and ended up in an Egyptian prison. Yet God had given him a dream and a promise of prosperity and leadership. God tested his confidence in His word. "The word of the Lord tested him." Psalm 105:19. Sometimes, when God gives us a promise, things can get worse before they get better. Are we being tested?

In Hebrews, we read not to cast away our confidence, followed by *"For you have need of endurance, so that after you have done the will of God, you may receive the promise."* Hebrews 10:36. We need endurance to match our confidence.

Our faith and confidence will be tested. When we went to PNG to start a Bible College, we were promised that College accommodation and a house would be ready. However, when we arrived, we found the college accommodation was only half completed, and the foundation for our home had yet to be laid.

So, we started the College up in the hills at a run-down Scout Camp for three months until the College accommodation was ready in Port Moresby. We were surrounded by jungle and mosquitoes. It was hot and humid, with no fans or air conditioning.

While our house was being built, as a family, we became vagabonds for twelve months, moving from "leave-house" to "leave-house." A "leave-house" became vacant when people went on leave. They would want someone living in their house for security as the crime rate for "break-and-entry" was horrendous in Port Moresby.

It was a tough time for us as a family. My wife Caroline and the children were excellent, but we could have easily cast away our confidence, spat the dummy, and returned to Australia.

However, we endured and never lost confidence in God's will and calling on our lives. After persevering, we finally moved into a house built on the same property as the College and Church. The College was a great success that impacted the nation. If we maintain our confidence and endure, we will be rewarded. "Therefore. do not cast away your confidence, which has great reward." Hebrews 10:35.

There are many Biblical examples of those who had unwavering confidence in God. There are too many to mention, but I will list a few -

Joshua and Caleb, the confident Israelites –

The Lord told Moses to send twelve spies to spy on the promised land. There was a difference of opinion when they returned and gave their report.

Joshua and Caleb demonstrated their faith and confidence in God. Caleb boldly said, *"Let us go up at once and take possession, for we are well able to overcome it."* Numbers 13:30.

However, the other ten spies gave a negative report,

implying it was impossible.

"But the men who had gone up with him said, "We are not able to go up against the people, for they are stronger than we." Numbers 13:31.

They declared that there were giants in the land and that they were like grasshoppers in their sight. This drained the people of faith and confidence. Joshua and Caleb spoke to the people again and tried to convince them to go in and possess the land, but they would not listen and wanted to stone them. As a result, the children of Israel wandered for forty years in the wilderness.

Joshua became Moses' assistant. After Moses died, God encouraged Joshua through His word, which gave him the confidence he needed to lead the people into the promised land.

"Have I not commanded you? Be strong and of good courage; do not be afraid, nor dismayed, for the Lord your God is with you wherever you go." Joshua 1:9. This is what Joshua needed to hear because he was well aware of the enemy in the land that they would have to drive out to possess it.

David, the confident Shepherd boy –

As a young shepherd boy, David showed incredible faith, courage and confidence in God when he faced Goliath, who had been mocking and intimidating the army of Israel. When David heard him, he was furious because Goliath was defying the armies of the living God. When he was to face Goliath, he said,

"The Lord, who delivered me from the paw of the lion and from the paw of the bear, He will deliver me from the hand of this Philistine." And Saul said to David, "Go and the Lord be with you." 1 Samuel 17:37.

Although David felled Goliath with a slingshot, his confidence was not in his ability with the slingshot but in God to deliver him just like He did from the lion and the bear while looking after the sheep.

Esther, the confident Queen –

Esther showed tremendous courage and confidence in risking her life to stand up for her people, the Jews, from a planned genocide. Haman was angry at Mordecai (Esther's cousin). He had refused to bow to him, so he convinced the King to issue a decree to annihilate all the Jews in the Persian Empire. When Mordecai tells Queen Esther, who is married to the king of this plot, she takes a risk and goes before the king to plead for her people.

She was bold and confident, saying, *"I will go to the king, which is against the law, and if I perish, I perish."* Esther 4:16. The king graciously accepted her request and sent Haman to the same gallows he had built for Mordecai.

The challenge for us today

Are we like those we have just mentioned, confident enough to defy the odds? When the Holy Spirit inspires us with a good

Seems Like a Good Idea

idea, we must be willing to move forward confidently despite the opposition we may face.

Chapter 15

A good idea needs the right timing

When we have a good idea to implement, our timing may never be perfect, but the right timing will save us a lot of unnecessary stress and anxiety if we misjudge it. As I have already said, we can end up embarrassed and discouraged because it seemed right, but we find out later that it did not work out because the timing was wrong.

It is crucial to get the timing right if we are making important decisions that will affect our future.

There is the story of a man who rushed into a railway station one morning and asked the ticket man, "When does the 8.01 train leave." "At 8.01" was the answer. "It is 7.59 by my watch, 7.57 by the town clock and 8.04 by the station clock." "Which clock should I go by?" The ticket man replied, "You can go by whichever you wish." But you cannot go by the 8.01 train because it has already left."

Some people think they can do things any time; if they procrastinate or are too early and do not consult God, they may miss His timing and the right train (opportunity).

God's timing is perfect

Have you ever wondered why Jesus came to this earth when He did? It was God's perfect timing.

"But when the right time came, God sent His Son." Galatians 4:4 (NLT). *Jesus was the right person, in the right place and time, to change the course of history. The rest of the passage explains that Jesus was born under the law to redeem those under it so they might become sons. God sent forth the Spirit of His Son into their hearts, crying out, "Abba, Father."*

Jesus issued an era of grace to introduce the gospel to all races and nations worldwide.

"For the law was given through Moses, but grace and truth came through Jesus Christ." John 1:17.

Yes, God's timing is perfect. You were no accident. You were born at the right time. Your challenge is to keep in step with Him.

Jesus knew the importance of timing

We are told that when Jesus drew near to the city of Jerusalem (probably descending from the Mount of Olives), He wept over it. (Luke 19:41). Why did He weep over Jerusalem?

He knew it would be destroyed prophetically in the future. (It was destroyed in 70 AD).

He said, *"Because you did not know the time of your visitation."* Luke 19:44.

Jerusalem was about to reject Christ the Messiah and crucify Him. They did not know the time of their visitation. Do we see the time of our visitation? How many people are lost because they have missed it? We want to take advantage of this opportunity to follow Christ and fulfil our calling and purpose.

Jesus knew He had to reach Jerusalem in time for the Passover; we read, *"He steadfastly set His face to go to Jerusalem."* Luke 9:51.

He needed to be present at the Passover, as He was to become the sacrificial Passover Lamb of God.

When Jesus stood before Pilate, *"It was the Preparation Day of the Passover."* John 19:14

When Jesus knew He was facing death by crucifixion, He wondered if there was some other way around it. But He knew it was His time. So, He prayed, *"Not My will but Yours be done."* Luke 19:42.

Nobody would look forward to dying by crucifixion, let alone death. We do not know when our time is up, but when that time comes, as Christians, we can look forward to the resurrection and eternal life.

The last leaf to fall from the tree

It is hard to predict when the last leaf will fall from the tree. When I was a boy, we had a deciduous apricot tree. During

Autumn, I would watch the leaves fall and try to guess which would be the last to fall from the tree as they changed from green to yellow to red. This process is called abscission or leaf fall.

Some trees' leaves were not designed to withstand the cold winter, but new leaves eventually replaced them in spring. This is a bit like our life-and-death cycle; when we die, others are born.

But we try to hang onto life as long as possible. Willie Nelson sings a song, *Last Leaf*, some of the lyrics convey this thought –

> *I'm the last leaf on the tree*
> *The Autumn took the rest*
> *But it won't take me*
> *I'm the last leaf on the tree*

Of course, this is not true. Hanging on to life as long as possible will not prevent us from falling. A woman recently told me she had a revelation on keeping a healthy body. She said, *"If we have faith, we do not have to carry sickness in our bodies,"* This is partially true, but she was implying that we do not have to die. Sounds good, but the Bible says, *"It is appointed for men to die once."* Hebrews 9:27.

We all have an appointment with death, but the good news is that Christians have eternal life in Christ. Our soul lives on; our body is laid to rest, but Jesus said believers never die. (John 11:26).

Our time frame should include eternity

Pursuing our good ideas on earth is only profitable if we include eternity on our agenda.

Making time for eternity should be our priority. We can spend all our time preparing for our future on earth, but if we do not know God, it is all in vain.

King Solomon, one of the wisest and wealthiest men who ever lived on earth, warns us that all is in vain without God in our lives. He explains that life is empty and pointless if we do not know God.

"Vanity of vanities, all is vanity. What profit has a man from all His labour in which he toils under the sun? One generation passes, and another comes." Ecclesiastes 1:2-3.

There is nothing wrong with prosperity, as God desires to bless us. However, what is the point if we lose our souls? After death, whatever profit or gain we have made remains, but our soul lives on for eternity in heaven or hell.

Jesus said, *"What does it profit a man if he gains the whole world and loses his own soul? "Or what shall a man give in exchange for his soul?"* Mark 8:36-37.

Your most valuable possession is your soul. What about you? Have you thought about your life's purpose and your soul's state? What will happen when you die? Are you prepared for eternity? All is vanity unless you are ready.

Believe in Jesus if you want assurance of eternal life. Jesus said to a Pharisee named Nicodemus, eager to be in the kingdom of God, *"You must be born again."* John 3:7. Jesus was speaking of a spiritual birth.

There is a time and a season for everything

Once you are prepared for eternity, you must realise that God has a plan and a purpose for your time on earth. There is a time and a season for everything.

> *"To everything, there is a season, a time for every purpose under heaven: a time to be born and a time to die."* Ecclesiastes 3:1-2. The following verses list many things that will possibly happen in our lifetime.

We may not have control over the timing of some of those things, but God wants us to focus on His time and purpose for our lives. He makes everything beautiful when it is within His time frame.

> *"He has made everything beautiful in its time. Also, He has put eternity in our hearts, except that no one finds out the work that God does from the beginning to the end."* Ecclesiastes 3:11.

We may not know the end from the beginning, and our timing may not be perfect, but it is beautiful when everything dovetails and is in harmony with God's timing. He makes everything beautiful in its time.

Make the most of your time on earth

You are encouraged to use your time wisely and take responsibility for your time on earth.

"Do not walk as fools but as wise, redeeming the time, because the days are evil. Therefore, do not be unwise, but understand the will of the Lord." Ephesians 5:15-17.

Discovering and pursuing God's will for our lives is crucial. If God is moving us in a specific direction, we need to know what it is and move with Him.

The council that met in Jerusalem (Acts 15) was timely as it sought God's will and wisdom to resolve the situation with the Jewish Christians demanding that the Gentiles be circumcised and abide by certain Jewish customs. The council was satisfied that it had discovered God's will and addressed the issue.

Investigate all the possibilities

Regarding timing, we need to be flexible and not force the issue. Some time ago, I had a minister say that he was going to go to such and such a place for a few years, whether God was in it or not. He went, and it was a disaster. The timing was all wrong, but God, in His mercy, restored the man and his ministry.

"Come now, you who say, "Today or tomorrow we will go to such and such a city, spend a year there, buy and sell and make a profit." However, you do not know what will happen tomorrow. For what is your life? It is even a vapour that appears for a little time and then vanishes away." James 4:13-14.

James warns us to be careful. We must get the timing right. How can we do this?

I have found it is wise to spy out the land before making a

life-changing decision. I had been on a ministry trip to PNG some twelve months before God called me to go there. So, I had some insight into understanding the people, culture, climate, and conditions.

After six years in PNG, we were invited to return to Australia to take over a church and Christian school in Lismore. To spy out the land, we flew back to Australia for a long weekend to take a church camp for Lismore some six months before accepting the invitation. So, we were familiar with the situation we were going to in Lismore.

The founder of On Your Path Consulting, Johanna Beyer, asks the question, "Does a redwood tree come out of the ground strong and tall and robust? No, growing and becoming majestic takes time and the right conditions." Her emphasis is on patience and timing. Johanna mainly works with people who feel unfulfilled with their current careers and are ready to create and accept a new challenge. Maybe you are at that point in your life.

Abraham and Sarah became impatient

We must believe in Divine timing. We know that God has a plan and a purpose for our lives. However, we can become impatient and feel pressured to make it happen ourselves. Abraham and Sarah had complained to God that they had no offspring. So, God challenged Abraham to believe.

> "Then God brought him outside and said, "Look toward heaven, and count the stars if you are able to number them." And He said to him, "So shall your descendants be". Genesis 15:3-5.

When they became impatient, they took things into their own hands. Sarah sent Abraham to their Egyptian maidservant Hagar so that she might bear a child for them. Hagar gave birth to Ishmael. But this was not a part of God's plan, as God had told Abraham that a son would come from his union with his wife, Sarah.

The timing was all wrong; they were forcing the issue well ahead of God. We must be careful not to take things into our own hands to produce something that seems like a good idea but is not what the Lord has planned for us.

However, in their old age, Sarah and Abraham eventually had a son God had promised, and they called him Isaac. God's blessing followed Isaac and his descendants.

The difference between Esau and Jacob

Esau and Jacob were twin sons born to Isaac and Rebekah. Even though they were twins, they were very different. Esau, being the firstborn, had certain privileges, including his birthright, a highly valued inheritance involving a double portion of the family wealth and status.

One day, Esau returned home exhausted from hunting in the field. He was tired and hungry. Jacob had prepared a stew. Esau was desperate and asked Jacob for some.

"And Esau said to Jacob, "Please feed me with that same red stew, for I am weary." Therefore, his name was called Edom. But Jacob said, "Sell me your birthright as of this day." And Esau said, "Look, I am about to die; so, what is this birthright to me?" Then Jacob said, "Swear to me

Seems Like a Good Idea

as of this day." So, he swore to him and sold his birthright to Jacob. And Jacob gave Esau bread and stew of lentils; then he ate and drank, arose and went his way. Thus, Esau despised his birthright." Genesis 25:30-34.

This was terrible timing for Esau, as he should have valued his birthright. But he despised it. I know some Christians and ministers with a calling upon their lives who have, in a way, done the same thing because of pride, a one-night stand, or mishandling finances. A friend in ministry used to say, "Watch out for the Girls, the Gold, and the Glory. They are traps the devil uses to tempt every man of God."

On the other hand, we can see that Jacob seized his opportunity to take advantage of Esau. Sure, Jacob means supplanter or deceiver. But he certainly timed his deception well and seized the moment.

The idea of seizing the moment was used in the movie *Dead Poets Society*, where the character John Keating, played by Robin Williams, encourages his students to make the most of their lives and embrace opportunities by saying "Carpe diem," Latin for "seize the day."

This is exactly what Jacob did. He seized the day—a day that changed history. God later changed Jacob's name to Israel. He eventually became the patriarch of the twelve tribes of Israel.

What can we learn from a spiritual point of view? Esau disregarded God's blessing in a moment of weakness and gave away his future inheritance. Jacob seized the moment, obtained the inheritance, and changed the course of history.

Enjoy the moments we have with people

When we engage with people, we should enjoy the moment by spending quality time with them.

We need to take an interest in the person we are engaging by asking questions, looking them in the eye, concentrating and conversing with them, and giving them more than a yes or no. Engage with them so they feel you care because you do.

I remember a senior minister with a high-profile ministry who would briefly engage with you, but while he was talking to you, he was not concentrating on you but looking around to see whom to talk to next. It is a trap we can easily fall into in ministry. When challenged about this, he said, "As the senior pastor, I want to get around as many people as possible." His motive was good, but you felt he was not enjoying the moment of engaging with you.

I have been guilty of this. My wife picked up on it and told me what I was doing. I was not aware of it until she told me. She is just the opposite. She gives someone her full attention. To some extent, I think it may be the difference between males and females.

In their book The Art of Possibility, Rosamund Stone Zander and Benjamin Zander said, "It's not about surviving; it's about allowing yourself to be touched by life and living in the present moment." They encourage us to take time to enjoy the moment.

Is your timing right?

Do you have the right time for your plans? When we need to make significant decisions like changing jobs, buying a house or a car, or choosing a church, we must have the right timing.

What about whatever seems to be a good idea for you? Is it ready for further investigation, exploration, and expansion? Does it seem inspired by the Holy Spirit and acceptable to you and others?

If so, step out in faith, and you will be surprised at what God can do with your good ideas. They may change the course of history.

Chapter 16

Was Jesus born to be a carpenter?

Have you ever wondered why you were born? Why you are who you are? Have you asked yourself, "What is my purpose in life?"

From a Christian perspective, discovering our God-given purpose in life helps us to have creative ideas that can change the course of history. There is no more significant example than Jesus and His disciples.

It would seem that Jesus knew early on that He was not born to be a carpenter. He lived and worked as a carpenter but was not born to be one. His God-given purpose was revealed as He began His public ministry. Being a carpenter was essential to growing up and maturing for ministry.

When Jesus was about thirty years old, He stood up in the synagogue, and when it was His turn, He read from the Book of Isaiah.

"The Spirit of the Lord is upon Me to preach the gospel to the poor; He has sent me to heal the broken hearted, to proclaim liberty to the captives and recovery of sight to the blind, to set at liberty those that are oppressed; to proclaim the acceptable year of the Lord." Luke 4:18-21.

All eyes were fixed on Him, waiting for what He would say about the scripture He had just read. He said to them, *"This day is this scripture fulfilled in your hearing."* They were stunned and said, *"Is not this Joseph's son?"* (the carpenter). But Jesus had just revealed His God-given ministry and purpose.

Soon after this, Jesus began to fulfil what he had just read. As the Son of God, He preached the gospel; he forgave sinners, healed all those oppressed by the devil, cast out demons, opened blind eyes, and caused the lame to walk.

The overall ministry of Jesus is summed up beautifully in Acts 10:38. *"How God anointed Jesus of Nazareth with the Holy Spirit and with power, who went about doing good and healing all who were oppressed by the devil, for God was with Him."*

Before His crucifixion, when Jesus' earthly ministry ended, He stood before Pilate, who said to Him, *"Are you a king then?" "Jesus answered," "You say rightly that I am a king. For this cause, I was born, and for this cause, I have come into the world, that I should bear witness to the truth. Everyone who is of the truth hears My voice."* John 18:37.

So, here we have Jesus revealing his eternal purpose. When asked if He was a king, He said, *"For this purpose I was born."* He was not born to be a carpenter but a king. The Bible declares that He is coming again as the King of kings and the Lord of lords (Revelation 19:16). Even though He grew up as a carpenter, He was not born to be a carpenter.

What about the disciples of Jesus?

We could say the same about the disciples. They were from different backgrounds; we know Matthew was a tax collector, but we are only told about the others who were fishermen.

"And as He walked by the Sea of Galilee, He saw Simon and Andrew, his brother, casting a net into the sea; for they were fishermen. Then Jesus said to them. "Follow Me, and I will make you fishers of men." They immediately left their nets and followed Him. When they had gone a little farther from there, He saw James, the son of Zebedee, and John, his brother, who also were in the boat mending their nets. And immediately He called them, and they left their father Zebedee with the hired servants and went after Him." Mark 1:16-20.

Were they born to be fishermen? Well, not according to Jesus. He called them to be fishers of men. *"Follow Me, and I will make you fishers of men,"* Jesus called them to follow Him and eventually fish for men by becoming disciples, apostles, and preachers of the gospel.

Your future is still unwritten

Only God knows the future, but we make the choices that shape our future. This is portrayed in the song "Unwritten" by Natasha Bedingfield. Some of the lyrics reflect the truth that we hold the pen and, to some extent, write the script.

"I'm just beginning, the pens in my hand, ending unplanned" "Live your life with arms wide open; today is where your book begins; the rest is still unwritten."

No matter what your life has been up until now, you can make decisions that will determine your future.

We are all born for a purpose

We were all born for a purpose. It takes time to discover that purpose, but first and foremost, God calls you to become a Christian, regardless of your nationality, race or ethnic upbringing.

Denzel Washington says, "I was not put on this earth to be an actor." "I was put on this earth to share and to be an example of God's power, wisdom, grace, and mercy in my life."

The Jews and Gentiles, the council in Jerusalem discussed in Acts 15, were both under the New Covenant and were accepted in Christ by the grace of God and not their Jewish customs.

Paul expounds on how the message of the cross applies to both Jews and Gentiles.

"For the message of the cross is foolishness to those who are perishing, but to us who are being saved, it is the power of God." 1 Corinthians 1:18.

Jews and Gentiles were reminded that it was the cross of Christ and His shed blood that made them one. They are now called Christians. But why did this seem to be foolish to those who were non-Christians?

"For Jews request a sign, and Greeks seek after wisdom, but we preach Christ crucified to the Jews a stumbling block and to the Greeks foolishness, but to those who are called, both Jews and Greeks, Christ the power of God and the wisdom of God. 1 Corinthians 1:22-24.

The Jews were interested in power, whereas the Greeks were more interested in wisdom.

So, the message of the cross made little sense to both Jews and Greeks because it seemed to nullify what they were both looking for until they had a revelation of salvation through the blood of Christ shed on the cross and the grace of God toward the whole human race.

It is the same for us today. No matter our nationality, we must embrace the message of the cross so we can be born again. This is what it means to be a Christian: to be born again and made new by God, not through our good deeds or participation in religious rituals, but through trusting in Jesus—in His death, which takes the judgment for our sins, and in His resurrection, which gives us new life. Only after becoming Christians can we discover our God-given purpose.

What is your God-given purpose?

This raises the question, "What were you born to be?" "What is your real purpose in life?"

Most people have a survival mindset. They think they are here to work, earn wages, eat, and stay alive; this becomes a cycle for many people. They work to earn wages, to eat, to stay alive, to work, to earn wages, to eat, to stay alive, to work. I have deliberately repeated myself because many people are on this treadmill with no other purpose in life. Although this may be true, we believe we have a God-given purpose as Christians.

However, we live in a world where people are so busy that some feel guilty that they do not measure up if they are not more meaningfully involved in church life. I have heard people complain because they seem to think the church makes them feel unworthy for their lack of involvement. But this is a guilt trip, and it is up to the individual to figure out what they can do.

However, applying the thought, "Jesus was not born to be a carpenter," to your own life may mean you were born to do more than your current work. There may be a purpose to your life that you have not yet discovered.

Some guidelines -

Here are some guidelines that may help you. -

1. Make it a matter of prayer
2. Read and study the scriptures.
3. Discover your passion and giftings
4. What have life experiences taught you so far?
5. Watch for open doors and opportunities.
6. Do you have confirmation?
7. Does it give you a sense of peace?
8. Seek the right timing.
9. Step out in faith.

Chapter 17
Step out in faith and have a go

Some Australians would say, "Have a go, mate." This colloquial Australian expression encourages someone to step out in faith, try something new, and take risks. It is often used to inspire someone to do something rather than sit and do nothing.

The late Clark Taylor was a high-profile ministry in Australia some years ago. As he puts it, he was a bloke from the bush who had been converted as a farmer and a stockman in the Outback. To use another colloquial Australian expression, Clark was a "Fair dinkum Aussie." He led Christian Outreach Churches and embarked on a church planting program.

When younger men approached him, looking for ministry, he often pointed them in a specific direction and said, "Step out in faith, and have a go, mate." They usually did, and many were successful.

In her book *Daring Greatly*, Brene Brown quotes a part of a famous speech by Theodore Roosevelt.

"It is not the critic who counts, not the man who points out how the strong man stumbles or where the doer of deeds could have done them better. The credit belongs to the man who is actually in the arena, whose face is marred by dust and sweat and blood, who strives valiantly...who at best knows, in the end, the triumph of high achievement, and who at worst, if he fails, at least fails while daring greatly."

Yes, it is not the critic who counts but the one who is in the arena - the one who is prepared to step out in faith and have a go, and if he fails, at least he fails while daring greatly.

If we have what seems to be a good idea, we need the faith and courage to implement it, step out, and have a go.

I once heard a minister devalue missionaries by saying negatively that Sunday School teachers qualify for the mission field, and they should be sent out to do the job. I was not sure of his motive, but it was easy for him to be sarcastic when he was living in his lovely air-conditioned home, driving a new car, eating at luxurious restaurants, and preaching to his wealthy congregation – while his so-called Sunday School teaching Missionaries were risking their lives daily, living in a foreign country in hot and humid conditions (or freezing), surviving on local food, and preaching to the poor and needy while trying to raise funds to survive. Which one was in the arena marred by dust, sweat and blood? Sure, to be fair, they were both serving God in different arenas. But that is no excuse to belittle missionaries, as one ministry is just as valuable as the other.

Why sit here until we die?

Instead of daydreaming while we grow old and sitting around doing nothing, we often miss opportunities to step out in faith and have a go.

The Bible tells us there was a time of severe famine in Samaria, the capital city of the northern kingdom of Israel. The city had been under siege by the Syrians, and the people were suffering terribly from starvation. They became so desperate for food that they sold and ate donkey's heads and dove's dung. A woman told the king how she agreed with another woman to eat her son, and then they would eat the other woman's son the next day. So, they boiled and ate her son, but the other woman hid her son the next day.

While these terrible things were happening to people starving in the city, four lepers were outcasts because of their disease. They were starving as they sat outside the entrance gate to the city, trying to decide what to do about their situation.

"Why are we sitting here until we die?" "If we say, 'We will enter the city,' the famine is in the city, and we shall die there. And if we sit here, we die also. Now, therefore, come, let us surrender to the army of the Syrians. If they keep us alive, we shall live; and if they kill us, we shall only die." 2 Kings 7:3-4.

They said, *"Why are we sitting here until we die?"* What a great question. I wonder how many people are doing that without even realising it when they could have tried something or at least died "daring greatly." What about you? If God has put something on your heart, why not get up in faith and have a go?

It seemed like a good idea

The lepers must have thought going to the enemy camp was a good idea. They might get fed or die; they were dying anyway, so they had nothing to lose.

When they arrived at the enemy's camp, it was utterly deserted. Unbeknown to them, God had caused the Syrians to hear the sound of a great army approaching, which made them flee in terror, thinking Israel had hired a foreign army. They fled, leaving all their food, supplies and wealth behind.

The lepers entered the tents, ate and drank, and took silver, gold and clothing. However, they realised that people were starving back in the city. So, they decided to return and tell the king the good news.

"Then they said to one another, "We are not doing right. This day is a day of good news, and we remain silent. If we wait until morning light, some punishment will come upon us. Now, therefore, come, let us go and tell the king's household. 2 Kings 7:9.

When this news spread, the people rushed out of the city to the enemy camp and were saved from starving.

When we have good news that can save people's lives, will we wait until we die, or will we step out in faith and have a go? It might be to share our faith with somebody who needs to hear the gospel.

We read in Ezekiel that if the watchman sees the sword coming and does not warn the people, God holds the watchman responsible for the people's blood. (Ezekiel 33:6). The apostle Paul probably has this in mind when he says, *"I am innocent of the blood of all men." "For I have not shunned to declare to you the whole counsel of God."* Acts 20:26-27. Jesus also calls us to be witnesses to Him. (Acts 1:8)

A change of attitude

The lepers had a change of attitude, going from hopelessness to "Why sit here until we die?" "Let's go to the enemy camp and see what will happen." It was a "Let's have a go" attitude. We have nothing to lose. We could say that if we die, we die "daringly."

"In my book *Enjoying Your Twilight Years*, I devote a whole chapter to "Watching your Attitude." It has to do with how we think, feel and act, usually in that order. Psychologists define attitude as "A learned tendency to evaluate things in a certain way, including evaluations of people, issues, objects, or events."

Your attitude is something you can change. It is not permanent. It can be changed by the influence of our circumstances and the positive attitude of others around us. The four lepers would have challenged one another to have a positive attitude and believe in a good outcome.

In his book Man's Search for Meaning, Viktor Frankl says, "When we are no longer able to change a situation, we are challenged to change ourselves."

You need the courage to do something you want instead of just daydreaming about it and sitting around doing nothing.

Seems Like a Good Idea

Some years ago, I was daydreaming about chartering a self-drive boat to cruise around the beautiful Whitsunday Islands off the coast of Queensland, Australia. These islands are unique. They are rugged and mountainous, with plenty of sheltered anchorages and white sandy beaches fringed by coral reefs and various fish. Captain James Cook discovered them on Whit Sunday (the day of Pentecost) in 1770.

I decided to hire a 35-foot cruiser to accommodate the family. Up until that point, I had only driven a little tinnie. Everybody said I was crazy because I knew nothing about cruisers, navigation, or the Whitsunday Islands.

But after studying maps and videos, I decided to "give it a go." It was not all plain sailing but one of the most exciting, adventurous, and meaningful holidays we have ever experienced. It was so good that we did it again a few years later.

If I had chosen to sit at home and daydream, that would have been all I had: a daydream.

Crossing the line

In his booklet *Cross the Line*, Sam Parker, co-founder of "Inspire Your People," states – "The Idea: with everything, there's a line. On one side of the line is a greater chance to make good things happen (better results, relationships, more opportunities). When you cross the line separating failure from success, you'll discover that not everyone will applaud your choice. Unfortunately, sometimes those people might be your friends. Nor will everything go your way. To cross the line is to commit, work hard, focus, and bounce back when things get tough."

From a Christian perspective, we could probably put it this way: To cross the line, we need to step out in faith and have a go rather than sit and do nothing. If we are prepared to do this, we are putting our faith into action.

"Thus, if it does not have works, faith is dead. But someone will say, "You have faith, and I have works. Show me your faith without works, and I will show you my faith by my works." James 2:17-18. (I will show you my faith by my actions).

James says you can tell me you have faith, but I want to see it through your works (or actions). Otherwise, your faith is dead, achieving nothing.

Faith in action is an outward expression of what is in our hearts by way of faith that causes us to care for the needy, show loving kindness, uphold justice, and serve others according to the teachings of Jesus.

"My little children, let us not love in word or tongue but in, deed and in truth." 1 John 3:18.

We walk by faith, not by sight

When we step out in faith and "have a go", we do not know the end from the beginning like God. He often reveals His plans to us on a "need-to-know" basis, and God determines who needs to know and when. It would be much easier if we could see the complete picture. This is why the Bible says, *"For we walk by faith, not by sight."* 2 Corinthians 5:7.

The fact that the council in Jerusalem (Acts 15) had to come together to pray and discuss the issue of the Gentiles coming to faith in Christ and how to handle it proves my point. They did not receive a direct email from God. They did not require certainty. They were happy to go ahead with what "seemed" pleasing to the Holy Spirit and those gathered together. God sees the big picture, but for us, it unfolds as we step out in faith.

This can be frustrating as we usually like to know how things will turn out in advance. In His wisdom, maybe God keeps some things hidden from us, and if we know too much, we may never step out in faith and "have a go."

Let His peace be your umpire

When something "seems good" and brings peace to your heart and mind, it is usually a sign that you are moving in the right direction.

"And let the peace of God rule in your hearts, to which also you were called in one body, and be thankful." Colossians 3:15.

In this context, the Greek word for "rule" means to arbitrate or umpire. So, the peace of God indicates that we are on the right track as long as we let it rule our hearts. If we get off track, it is like a game where the umpire blows the whistle. When that happens, we must stop because we lose our peace and need to refocus.

Another great scripture tells us that the peace of God

surpasses our understanding. When we are unsure about things, we are told what to do.

"Be anxious for nothing, but in everything by prayer and supplication, with thanksgiving, let your request be made known to God; and the peace of God, which surpasses all understanding, will guard your hearts and minds through Christ Jesus." Philippians 4:6-7.

You may have something in your heart and be unsure whether to pursue it. Pray about it, investigate the possibilities, share your thoughts with someone, seek confirmation, and if it seems good and inspired by the Holy Spirit, then step out in faith and have a go.

If you have never given Christ a go, I encourage you to do so and invite Him into your heart to take control of your life.

I hope this book has inspired you to live the Christian life more effectively and that you will learn how to use the word "seemed" in conjunction with your good ideas and the leading of the Holy Spirit.

www.ingramcontent.com/pod-product-compliance
Lightning Source LLC
Chambersburg PA
CBHW031252290426
44109CB00012B/544